Questions & ~~Answers:~~

Finance

B Knight, P Morris and G Tapply

Croner Publications Ltd
Croner House
London Road
Kingston upon Thames
Surrey KT2 6SR
Telephone: 081-547 3333

Published by
Croner Publications Ltd
Croner House
London Road
Kingston upon Thames
Surrey KT2 6SR
Tel: 081-547 3333

While every care has been taken
in the writing and editing of this book,
readers should be aware that only Acts of Parliament
and Statutory Instruments have the force of law,
and that only the courts can authoritatively
interpret the law.

British Library Cataloguing in Publication Data
A CIP Catalogue Record for this book
is available from the British Library

ISBN: 1 85524 246 X

Printed by Whitstable Litho Ltd, Whitstable, Kent

THE AUTHORS

BRIAN KNIGHT has written extensively on educational finance since the late 1970s. His publications include *Managing School Finance* (1983 Heinemann), *Local Management of Schools* (1990 Longman) and *School Financial Management: The Thinking Manager's Guide* (1993 Heinemann), together with numerous articles. He has provided lectures and training on school financial management extensively in the UK and overseas.

He was previously Head of Holyrood School, Chard, and currently is an Honorary Research Fellow of the University of Exeter and an educational consultant.

PETER MORRIS is a retired teacher, having taught for 30 years in secondary schools. He is a governor of two schools in Humberside and has been Chairman of the National Association of Governors and Managers for the past two years.

GARY TAPPLY is an Education Finance Officer working in the Grimsby area of Humberside County Council, since 1989. His role is to provide support, advice and training in all aspects of financial management and administration to Heads and governing bodies of 80 schools. He was previously employed in the accountancy section at Great Grimsby Borough Council.

THE REVIEWERS

STEPHEN SZEMERENYI has been Head of Finchley Catholic High School since 1983; SHA council member since September 1989 and chairman of an LMS committee from 1991–93. He has written contributions for Croner's Head's and Governor's Briefings, SHA Headlines and the chapter entitled "Money Matters" in *Under New Management* published by Longman; has given frequent talks on LMS and run regular training courses; and sat on the steering committee of the LMS Initiative's "Study into Formula Funding" (provided by Coopers and Lybrand and the NFER) and of the Audit Commission report, *Adding up the Sums*.

JOHN WOOTON was Head of Liscard Primary School in Wallasey from 1969–1989 and was then seconded to the Wirral LEA until 1992, where his role was to support Heads and governing bodies in the implementation of LMS. From 1981–92 he served on the National Council of NAHT and was President in 1988/89. He has worked on a number of LMS projects, including the LMS Initiative produced by CIPFA, and has contributed articles to national publications. He now works as a consultant and is regularly involved in teacher and governor training.

INTRODUCTION

Most schools in England and Wales now have control over their own budgets. Many have enjoyed self-management of their finances for several years. Yet, although management of school finances becomes easier with experience, at the same time it is becoming more complex, for several reasons.

1. The rules of the game keep changing. Alterations are still frequently made by the DFE or by LEAs.
2. The full legal implications of LMS and GMS are only slowly becoming apparent, particularly in relation to some of the more hazardous areas such as compulsory competitive tendering, insurance, salary flexibilities, etc.
3. The need for more general principles to underpin pragmatic financial management is emerging. Common sense is not enough.

The authors and publisher therefore feel that this Question and Answer Book will answer many of the questions that Heads and governors are now asking, both at a legal and a conceptual level. We have tried to produce material suitable for all types of schools, but inevitably Heads of smaller primary schools may find some of the material needs to be adapted for their situation. However, we trust that the general principles will still be relevant for them.

QUESTIONS AND ANSWERS: FINANCE

(Supplementary questions are not listed)

ROLES AND STRUCTURES

Q1. What is the role of the governing body in school finance?

Q2. What is the structure of accountability for governing bodies and Heads?

Q3. Does the school have to appoint a finance committee?

Q4. What terms of reference should be given to a finance committee?

FORMULA FUNDING

Q5. What is formula funding?

Q6. What information on the funding formula must LEAs provide?

Q7. Are GM schools funded by formula and, if so, how?

Q8. How do cuts in formula funding actually affect educational provision?

THE BUDGET PROCESS

Q9. What are the functions of a budget?

Q10. What does the budget process involve?

Q11. How can a school consider the widest range of possible budget alternatives?

Q12. What is programme budgeting?

Q13. What is a base budget?

Q14. What is zero-budgeting?

THE BUDGET IN DETAIL

Q15.   What are the difficulties in linking the budget to the school development plan (SDP)?

Q17.   What is the ideal budget format?

Q18.   What use are unit costs?

Q19.   What is budget profiling?

Q20.   What are the advantages of budget profiling?

Q21.   What are the problems associated with budget profiling?

Q22.   What is the main aim of commitment accounting?

Q23.   How does the commitment accounting process work in practice?

Q24.   What are the best methods for allocating funds to internal budget-holders?

Q25.   How can the financial needs of curricular or other areas be assessed?

Q26.   How should non-public funds be dealt with?

Q27.   Who is responsible for arranging insurance cover?

Q28.   How can staff absence through injury or sickness be covered?

FACTORS AFFECTING THE BUDGET

Q29.   How can an inadequate allowance for inflation be identified?

Q30.   What is the effect of an inadequate allowance for inflation?

Q31.   Is it desirable to carry forward a surplus at the end of the financial year?

Q32.   Is it desirable to create a contingency fund?

Q33.   What are the fixed costs of a school?

Q34.   How does falling pupil enrolment affect a school's budget?

MISCELLANEOUS

SPECIAL EDUCATIONAL NEEDS

Q50. How should schools deal with special educational needs (SEN)?

Q51. What does the future hold for SEN funding?

PAY AND PERSONNEL

Q52. What is the position regarding pay flexibility?

Q53. Will performance related pay ever become a reality?

ASSOCIATE STAFF/VOLUNTEERS

Q54. What should the school bursar's role be?

Q55. How can imaginative use of associate (non-teaching) staff improve a school's cost-efficiency?

Q56. How can the value of volunteers be maximised?

Q57. How can pupils be involved in LMS?

CONTRACTS AND COMPULSORY COMPETITIVE TENDERING

Q58. What is compulsory competitive tendering (CCT)?

Q59. How does CCT affect maintained schools?

Q60. What is the case regarding CCT and GM or voluntary-aided schools?

Q61. What are the factors to take into account when purchasing and entering into contracts?

Q62. What are the procedures involved when purchasing or entering into contracts?

SPREADSHEETS

Q63. What is a spreadsheet?

Q64. What are the advantages of a spreadsheet?

Q65. What are the main uses of a spreadsheet?

TAX

Q66. In education, which goods and services are subject to Value Added Tax (VAT) and which are not?

Q67. How is VAT reclaimed?

Q68. What is the difference between input and output tax?

Q69. What is the Construction Industry Tax Deduction Scheme (CITDS)?

ROLES AND STRUCTURES

Q1. **What is the role of the governing body in school finance?**

A. The involvement of the governing body in the financial management of a school is determined by the Education Reform Act 1988:

- under s.33(1) LEAs have to prepare a scheme for the delegation of budget shares to schools maintained by them (maintained schools)

- s.36(2) places a duty on LEAs to put the budget share of each school at the disposal of its governing body to be spent for the purposes of the school subject to any provision made by or under the scheme

- s.36(5) entitles the governing body to spend the delegated budget as it sees fit and enables delegation of their powers to the Head in relation to any part of that sum, without incurring any personal liability, provided that they act in good faith

- s.37 deals with the withdrawal of delegation under certain circumstances, after giving not less than one month's notice, unless circumstances require LEAs to act sooner.

Similarly, under s.76(1), the Secretary of State is required to pay annual grants for the maintenance of grant-maintained (or self-governing) schools to the governing body of the school. Responsibility for financing GM schools will pass from Schools IV Branch of the Department for Education (DFE) to the new funding authorities to be set up under the Education Act 1993 which will be operating from April 1994.

Q2. **What is the structure of accountability for governing bodies and Heads?**

A.   The involvement of governing bodies in the financial management of schools is founded in law and Heads receive their delegated powers over the spending of the budget via the governing bodies. They are, therefore, accountable to their governing bodies.

Similarly, the governing body is accountable for the way the budget is managed to:

• the providers of the funds — the LEA in maintained schools and the Secretary of State in GM schools (until April 1994 when the funding authorities take over from Schools IV Branch of the DFE)

• the parents of pupils of the school — a financial statement must be provided with the annual report to parents, prior to the annual parents' meeting required by law

• the wider public — through those bodies set up to audit school finances to ensure probity and value for money.

Therefore, the ultimate responsibility for the management of the finances of the school rests with the governing body, but in order to avoid every governor being involved it is usual to devolve the day-to-day management of the budget to the Head and to set up a committee of the governing body to monitor spending and to assist the Head.

For maintained schools the Director of Finance (or a representative) of the LEA has the right to attend meetings of the governing body for the purpose of providing financial advice and support.

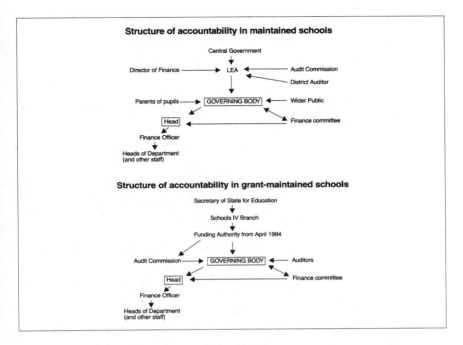

Structure of accountability in maintained schools

Central Government

Director of Finance → LEA ← Audit Commission
← District Auditor

Parents of pupils → GOVERNING BODY ← Wider Public

Head ← Finance committee

Finance Officer

Heads of Department
(and other staff)

Structure of accountability in grant-maintained schools

Secretary of State for Education

Schools IV Branch

Funding Authority from April 1994

Audit Commission → GOVERNING BODY ← Auditors

Head ← Finance committee

Finance Officer

Heads of Department
(and other staff)

NB Finance Officer — the member of school staff responsible for monitoring the spending of the school budget share. Some secondary schools have appointed a bursar or school manager. In the primary sector the Head usually assumes this responsibility and this may result in the appointment of extra staff to relieve the Head from some or all of his or her teaching commitments.

In GM schools a transitional grant is available to schools (based on a bid). The money is typically spent taking on a financial manager, sorting out payroll and contractual matters and purchasing office equipment.

Q3. Does the school have to appoint a finance committee?

A.   For maintained schools there is no legal requirement, although it is usual, to establish a finance committee, but in GM schools the articles of government require the governing body to appoint one.

Appointments to the finance committee are normally made annually at the first meeting of each new academic year when the membership of all committees is decided.

Q4. What terms of reference should be given to a finance committee?

A.   The terms of reference for the finance committee are determined by the governing body and should be modified and/or confirmed annually.

In deciding the terms of reference the governing body should have regard to two principles:

- to allow the Head to get on with the job of the day-to-day running of the school, and

- to ensure the control and monitoring of the school budget.

The avoidance of undue interference is of prime importance and this can only come from an attitude of mutual trust.

Terms of reference should include *all* of the following:

- to consider and advise the governing body on the financial implications of adopting certain policies, especially those with long-term budget implications

- to interpret and implement the broad policies of the governing body in so far as they involve financial matters

- to take decisions on financial matters that need to be dealt with between meetings of the governing body which may be cash limited (see below)

- to provide information and reports so as to enable the governing body to comply with the financial regulations set down by the providers of the funds to the school

- to monitor the progress of expenditure during the year (the Audit Commission recommends that governors should receive, at least on a termly basis, a report on expenditure and the budget)

- to prepare a draft budget, with recommendations as necessary, on projections of income and expenditure for the governing body as a whole to consider and decide upon.

The governing body may feel that limits must be set to restrict the amount spent by the Head. Similarly, it may decide that items of expenditure costing above a certain value must be referred back to it.

The finance committee will need to meet more often than the governing body and must produce minutes for examination by the whole governing body.

FORMULA FUNDING

Q5.   What is formula funding?

A.   Schools covered by the LEA scheme for LMS receive a
        budget share which is determined by the application of a
        formula devised by the LEA, and approved by the Secretary
        of State for Education contained within the submission
        required under s.42 of the Education Reform Act 1988.
        From April 1993 all schools should be included in a scheme,
        except for special schools which should be included from
        April 1994 and must be included from April 1996. Even
        though the framework for s.42 statements laid down in the
        DES Circular 7/88 gives precise guidance, and the regula-
        tions contained in the Education (School Financial State-
        ments) Regulations 1993 (SI 1993 No. 113) prescribe the
        particulars required, LEAs have sufficient discretion to en-
        sure that there will be almost as many schemes as there
        are LEAs and the formula will not always be reduced to
        algebraic form. The school budget share of the potential
        schools' budget (PSB) will be arrived at largely based on
        the number of pupils in each school weighted for differ-
        ences in age (age weighted pupil units (AWPUs)) and will
        take account of the objective needs rather than historical
        bases.

**Q6.   What information on the funding formula must
        LEAs provide?**

A.   LEAs must produce information about the funding formula
        and provide a detailed explanation by 31 March of each
        year. This LEA annual financial statement is required under
        s.42 of the Education Reform Act 1988. Failure to produce
        it on time could result in the GM schools in an area taking

more than their share of the cash available for all funded schools.

The basic format of the statement (see the box below) has been determined by the Secretary of State and must be made available for public inspection at LEA offices and public libraries.

Basic format of the funding formula statement

- Part 1 of the statement gives details of the overall planned expenditure, either directly or indirectly, on primary and secondary schools, ie the general schools' budget (GSB). It also gives details of the expenditure not devolved to schools.
- Part 2 analyses expenditure and gives details of the schools' budget shares.
- Part 3 explains the formula used to calculate the schools' budget shares and gives details of the amount per pupil, which varies according to age. The formula also includes elements for a block sum depending on school size (providing protection for small schools) in terms of premises related costs, special needs and salaries, etc. There may also be an element for enabling the transition of schools to delegated budgets; this may only last for four years from the inception of the LMS scheme.
- Part 4 shows how the formula has been applied for each school within the LMS scheme.

Education Budget

less non-school items

General Schools' Budget (GSB)

less mandatory exceptions and DFE named discretionary

exceptions

Potential Schools' Budget (PSB)

less discretionary exceptions (15% limit 93/94/95: 10% 95/96 onwards)

Aggregate Schools' Budget (ASB)

divided among schools by formula

Budget Share of Each School

From April 1993, at least 85% of the potential schools' budget (PSB) must be delegated to schools; 80% of which must be based on age weighted pupil numbers.

From April 1995 at least 90% of the PSB will have to be delegated to schools. (85% delegation in inner-London from April 1995 — 90% from 1996.)

Q7. Are GM schools funded by formula and, if so, how?

A.　Yes. The budget data required by DFE from LEAs under s.42 of the Education Reform Act 1988 is important in that it determines, to a large extent, the level of funding for GM schools. Funding is achieved through a system of grants which are formula based.

When a school is approved for GM status the governing body receives a *transitional grant* as a one-off payment to enable the changeover to GM status to take place. Currently, this amounts to £30,000 plus £30 for each pupil (up to a maximum of £60,000) for schools with 200 or more pupils; and £20,000 plus £30 per pupil for schools with fewer than 200 pupils. It meets essential extra spending and is typically spent on taking on a financial manager, sorting payroll problems and purchasing office equipment.

The *annual maintenance grant* (AMG), recoverable from the LEA, is made up of:

- a *direct* element, which is the amount the school would have received had it still been maintained by the LEA
- a *central* element, which is provided to buy in those services that LEA schools receive "free" (a percentage addition to the direct AMG is calculated separately for each LEA since delegation varies from one LEA to another)
- a *meals* element, which adds on 1–2% of the direct AMG
- in addition, expenditure on nursery education or on statemented pupils previously paid for by the LEA is also now due to the school.

The AMG is paid in 13 instalments, including two in April.

Other *special purpose grants* are available for:

- curriculum and staff development (£42.50 per pupil)
- VAT (2.5% of the AMG, but less for ex-maintained schools due to the rate reduction on automatically acquiring charity status when becoming GM)
- premises insurance (50% of premiums to a maximum of £6000)
- staff restructuring, which covers premature retirement, redundancy and voluntary severance (for one year after becoming GM, schools can apply for a one-off payment, subject to bidding, for restructuring of staff).

Two kinds of *capital grant* are available to GM schools: one based on a formula of £11,000 plus £20 per pupil and the other for named projects for which bids must be made (projects connected with health and safety, technology and science receive priority allocation).

GM schools continue to be eligible for Section 11 funding and Technical and Vocational Education Initiative (TVEI) support.

A future development to fund GM schools on a *common funding formula* is still under general consultation and is expected to be introduced as a pilot scheme in some selected areas in 1994. More detailed consultation will take place in the selected areas prior to the scheme's introduction.

A useful publication in this area is *GM Schools in England: Financial Controls* (1993, HMSO).

Q8. **How do cuts in formula funding actually affect educational provision?**

A. At first sight the answer is obvious: reduced funding equals reduced expenditure. However, the actual effect of reduced funding is complex. (The reduced funding may arise from budget cuts or from a change in the formula which affects a school adversely.)

First, a significant proportion of a school's costs cannot be easily reduced over the short term to respond to a cut in funding. These "non-reducible costs" include, for example, the Head's salary, allocated spine points, some support staff salaries, energy costs, cleaning services, grounds maintenance, examination fees (secondary schools) and all items on fixed contracts. This will amount to 20–25% of total costs for most schools and will be higher in schools which are operating significantly below capacity. So any cuts will fall upon the 75–80% "reducible costs". (Note that "non-reducible costs" should not be confused with "fixed costs", which are costs which do not alter when pupil numbers alter, although, obviously, there is considerable overlap — see Question 33.)

Second, when schools are faced with cuts they tend to reduce certain categories of expenditure more than others. They will be reluctant to reduce the number of teaching or support staff employed. (Reductions cannot be made in individual salaries where there is a legal entitlement to it, unless relating to an additional payment which is not of a permanent nature.) They will find it difficult to make major economies in energy, establishment expenses (advertise-ments, interviews, travelling and subsistence), telephone and postage costs. So pressure is likely to fall on areas where a reduction *can* be made and where the immediate effect will not be apparent. The most obvious examples are books, equipment (and to a lesser extent stationery and materials), furniture, building maintenance and redecora-tion, and in-service training. The latter all have a common feature: if purchased in year 1 they are all "consumed" over the next few years. So a cut in year 1 does not affect the stock of unconsumed goods or services still existing from purchases in previous years.

Therefore, a cut in these areas will have less immediate effect than might be expected. For example, if a school's book stock has an average life of five years, then if the school cuts out all book purchases for one year, at the end of the year it would still have 80% of its book stock. Similarly, an embargo on redecoration will often only have a marginal immediate effect.

The disadvantage is that the effect of a cut in these areas lingers on. The book stock would remain at an 80% level for another four years and redecoration will be at the reduced level for the whole of one redecoration cycle.

Even a small cut in funding will be heavily concentrated in particular areas, leading to severe long-term problems.

THE BUDGET PROCESS

Q9. **What are the functions of a budget?**

A.   A budget is one of those items which is taken for granted because of its familiarity — it is often seen simply as a statement of planned expenditure against which actual expenditure can be matched.

A much wider range of functions have, however, been identified and include the following:

- planning
- forecasting
- matching expenditure to income
- establishing priorities
- comparing the value of alternatives
- implementing plans
- co-ordinating school activities
- allocating resources
- authorising expenditure and activities
- communicating objectives to personnel
- motivating personnel by delegation
- controlling expenditure
- strengthening accountability
- obtaining value for money, economising
- matching inputs against outcomes.

So a budget is a *multi-purpose management tool*, adaptable for different purposes. The presentation of budget material for planning, for example, needs to be quite different from that for implementation, and control and monitoring; while the presentation for evaluation against actual outcomes needs to be different again. Also, a budget is not just concerned with expenditure. You can only spend against projected income, and so as schools move more into generating their own funds, the projected income side of the budget will become increasingly important.

Q10. What does the budget process involve?

A. The budget process for a particular financial year actually spreads over nearly two years, in four main stages.

1. *Preliminary analysis (early part of the academic year).* Here the objectives and priorities of the school development plan (SDP) are introduced; alternatives for their delivery considered and costed; and early projections for the coming financial year and their implications discussed.

2. *Construction (before the new financial year).* As more detailed information becomes available on likely outcomes of the previous budget, the new delegated budget total, projected enrolment, staff changes and salary/price rises, etc, draft budgets can be constructed, leading to a final version for the governors' approval.

3. *Control and monitoring (during the academic year).* Once the year begins, actual expenditure needs to be monitored against the intended expenditure — and controlled to ensure that expenditures are properly authorised and subject to audit controls.

4. *Evaluation (after the end of the financial year).* This involves evaluating the final expenditure situation and, more importantly, matching this against intended objectives and actual outcomes.

Generally speaking, schools entering LMS have been quick to master the middle two stages. They have found the other stages more difficult. In preliminary analysis they have not always found linkage with the SDP easy (see Question 15) and have not always developed systems for looking at and costing the widest possible range of alternative strategies (see the following question). Similarly, while they have normally found the immediate evaluation of the final budget statement (often called "month 13") straightforward, they have found deeper evaluation rather more difficult (see Question 40).

> For an extended and thoughtful examination of the budget process, see Simkins T and Lancaster D, *Budgeting and Resource Allocations in Educational Institutions* (Sheffield Polytechnic 1987, Paper in Educational Management 35). Obtainable from the Centre for Educational Management, Sheffield Hallam University, 36 Collegiate Crescent, Sheffield S10 2BP. There is also a useful practical NAHT booklet, *Budget Setting Principles*.

Q11. How can a school consider the widest range of possible budget alternatives?

A.   Suppose a school has an objective within its SDP "to improve substantially the performance of the bottom 20% lowest achieving pupils". Logically, to translate this into the budget the school should consider the fullest possible range of alternative methods to achieve this objective, and select the one or ones which seem most likely to be cost-effective.

In this particular situation many schools would consider strategies such as:

- improving the pupil-teacher ratio (PTR)
- providing additional support staff in class
- funding individual and small group withdrawal teaching, and
- improving the learning resources used and the school library.

But the actual strategies examined will often be far less than the full range available.

In this example the school could have considered:

- an incentive allowance and time for teachers to develop improved learning materials
- greater use of computer-assisted learning and new educational technology
- an INSET programme for all staff on low achieving pupils
- the appointment of a home-school liaison worker to improve parent support for low achievers
- an extended day/twilight clinic programme
- individual coaching outside the school day
- the appointment of an organiser to lead a team of volunteer tutors, as in adult literacy programmes
- intensive holiday "catch-up" schemes
- the appointment of an organiser for an extensive peer-tutoring scheme, with older pupils helping younger low achievers
- personal counselling for low achievers.

Often schools would not consider a range of alternatives as wide as this to meet the original objective (and the above list is by no means exhaustive) — particularly those lower down on the list. Yet some of the options, eg peer-tutoring, are low cost, so they only need to show small returns to be cost-effective.

So how can schools open up a wider range of alternatives to be considered for inclusion in the budget? Three requirements may be needed:

- a climate within the school which encourages innovative and free-ranging thinking

- a structured procedure for identifying the fullest range of alternatives — perhaps an organised "brain-storming" session

- an awareness of the political dimension which tends to focus attention on teacher and material-centred strategies and to resist consideration of less traditional approaches (eg some of those at the lower end of the list above).

Once a wider range of strategies has been identified, these will each need rough costings and assessment for their likely effectiveness.

Q12. What is programme budgeting?

A.　Programme budgeting was first popularised as PPBS (the Planning Programming Budgeting System), introduced by President Lyndon Johnson into the US Government. It is a very logical approach to budgeting, based upon a trenchant critique of the conventional budgetary system whereby budgets are built up on a "line-item" basis, category by category, without any specific linkage to objectives or to an assessment of the extent to which the objectives have been achieved.

The logic for programme budgeting is very strong and for a time PPBS had a very high profile in the USA. In education it was used extensively by school boards, although not much in schools themselves. However, it had two serious disadvantages:

- it was much more time-consuming than the traditional method, with extensive documentation

- it still needed to be converted into a line-item budget for effective expenditure monitoring and control.

So, in the USA it has now largely died out, and almost totally so in education.

Programme budgeting has, however, recently had a revival in Australia, this time at the school level and in a revised form. Many schools in the state of Victoria now use this, as do charter schools in New Zealand.

Under the revised system, the school identifies a range of perhaps 12–40 "programmes", eg subjects, special needs, other school activities (extra-curricular, etc), premises and grounds, PR and marketing, etc. The financial needs of each are then identified for staffing (teaching and support), premises, supplies and services, and then the budget of all the programmes are collated into a master budget. This is then reconciled with the funds available.

It remains to be seen whether this new form of programme budgeting will survive better than its PPBS predecessor. It is certainly more logical than the traditional budget construction, but it is also much more time-consuming and so may eventually lose popularity or be simplified.

Q13. What is a base budget?

A.   This approach to budget construction was developed by the Audit Commission. The concept is simple. First, the school builds up its budget *on the most niggardly basis possible* — the tightest staffing, teaching and non-teaching requirements, and the least conceivable expenditure on premises, supplies and services. This then becomes the *base budget*, while the remainder of the delegated budget is the *discretionary budget*.

The advantage of the base budget approach is that it challenges the status quo without the time-consuming "building from the bottom up" of programme budgeting. It accepts that a school has substantial ongoing expenditure which is inherent in its function, but attempts to minimise this and so encourage more flexible thinking at the margins.

However, the base budget approach has its limitations.

- It works best where schools are either LMS budget gainers or in more generously funded LEAs. (In LMS loser schools or schools in very constrained LEAs, there may not be enough freedom in the budget for this approach.)

- Even well-endowed schools often feel that their existing funding is at an absolute minimum, and so cannot see how a base budget can be constructed. In particular they often cannot see how their budget for teacher staffing can be reduced (but even marginal changes here can have a substantial effect — see Question 36). They need to think what would happen under an *extreme* cuts situation, as in a catastrophic economic crisis. What would be the absolute minimum on which they could still function as a school — that then will be their base budget.

- The temptation is to put back automatically into the discretionary budget anything which has been omitted from the status quo. This is a mistake — the discretionary budget should be used to explore the full range of possibilities with an open mind.

Despite — or perhaps because of — the Audit Commission's advocacy of the base budget, it does not seem to be widely used. It certainly deserves deeper consideration.

See Audit Commission's *Management within Primary Schools* (1991, HMSO) pp.23–25. Note that the concept can be adopted equally well in secondary schools.

Q14. What is zero-budgeting?

A. This concept was introduced by President Jimmy Carter into the US Government and is based on the idea that internal budget-holders should have no prior claim to funds and need to justify each year their claim to an allocation. Zero-budgeting is obviously valuable for challenging the status quo and cutting back the financial undergrowth. However, it is even more time-consuming than PPBS (see Question 12) because of its extensive paperwork, and it is also extremely threatening to budget-holders. Nowhere do schools currently operate it in its pure form.

Nevertheless the *concept* of zero-budgeting is very useful, particularly for looking at the allocation of the "development" aspects of the budget. It could also be used very effectively as part of a whole-school review.

THE BUDGET IN DETAIL

Q15. **What are the difficulties in linking the budget to the school development plan (SDP)?**

A.   In theory the SDP should be firmly linked to the budget. In practice many schools find this difficult because:

- the SDP will commonly have a three year span but it is difficult to plan financially beyond the next financial year, owing to uncertainty about funding
- the SDP, by definition, implies "development", but there may be little or no scope for development in the budget
- the SDP may involve proposals which have both a *developmental* and a *maintenance* aspect; the former may be one-off but the latter requires provision each year
- there may be several different plans — all with financial implications — operating under the SDP umbrella, eg curriculum development, human resource development and training, public relations and marketing, premises and grounds improvement, interaction with the community, or even a major development project, and each of these may have different time scales
- the SDP will be based on the academic year and the budget, obviously, on the financial year. This creates a particular problem, as shown below.

Linking your SDP to the budget

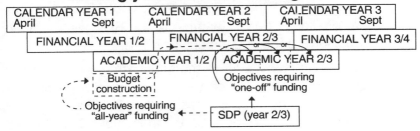

27

Here it is assumed that the second year of a school's SDP (calendar year 2/3) has needs for both *one-off* funding (eg improvements to premises or the purchase of books and equipment), and *all year* funding (eg salaries). Now the one-off funding (shown by the unbroken arrows) may be required for a specific time of the year, eg books in September, but may be appropriate at any time. Therefore, there may be flexibility in its timing, even between the financial years 2/3 and 3/4. All year funding, on the other hand, will be needed from the start of the academic year, so it must be in place in September of the financial year and must be inserted in the construction of the budget *early in the previous academic year*, ie 9–12 months before it is needed. Therefore, to implement this SDP for academic year 2/3, action has to be taken early in academic year 1/2.

See Hart J, *Successful Financial Planning and Management in Schools* (1993, Longman) for a fuller treatment of this planning budgeting linkage. For development plans, see *Planning for School Development* and *Development Planning: A Practical Guide* (1989 and 1991, HMSO).

Q16. How can these difficulties be overcome?

A.   By considering the answers to the following questions you should be able to ease the linkage problem and possibly solve it.

- Does your SDP, over years 1, 2 and 3, etc, have financial implications? (Many features of the SDP will not need additional or altered expenditure.)

- If so, how substantial is the finance required? You will have to calculate each year what percentage of your current spending on books, stationery, materials and equipment will be required to finance your SDP (the old "capitation"). If it is less than 10% you may well be able to fund this within the normal slack of the budget.

For example, in some schools the actual financial requirement of the SDP may be quite small, and here provision can be planned from term to term as suitable savings or virement become possible.

If not, and your SDP requirements are more than 10% of capitation, you will have to plan carefully. If your SDP requirements approach or exceed 100% of capitation, they imply a major project!

- Are large SDP requirements "one-off"?
- If they are, can they be provided for flexibly at any time? In this case you may be able to choose between two financial years for your provision, or spread the provision across both years — either way your task is easier.
- If, however, they *must* be provided at a particular time, or if they represent all-year expenditure, then they will need building in to your budget construction in the *previous* academic year, as shown in the diagram above.

Q17. What is the ideal budget format?

A.   The best budget format is the one which gives you the information that you *need*, not just the information that you *want*, because you may be unaware of what you need.

You need different information for the different stages of the budget process (for a fuller examination of these stages see Question 10). For example, for the analysis stage you need information about your objectives and your SDP (Question 15); about the alternatives available to you (Question 11); and provisional data on funding, enrolment and other budget factors.

For construction, control and monitoring you need a budget set out in the traditional line-item form. For monitoring and control you need regular progress reports to match actual expenditure against projected expenditure. LEA systems normally provide this information, with "spent to date", "projected expenditure to date" and "variance" columns. But for evaluation, apart from the final budget outcome, you need information on the success of programmes and developments, outcomes and achievements (see Question 40).

It is easier to sort out what information is needed if we look at the limitations of the budget format, as shown below. This example shows a format which is presented, with variations, to thousands of governing bodies every Spring as they approve their budgets.

Example of a budget format

GREENGLADES MIDDLE SCHOOL

Budget 1993–94 for Governors' approval

INCOME	£	£
Budget allocation (formula funded)	630,500	
Balance brought forward	24,320	
Income (estimated)	5,000	
TOTAL	659,820	659,820

EXPENDITURE		
Employees		
Teaching staff	460,280	
Supply cover	11,340	
Administration and support staff	65,830	
Mid-day supervisors	13,470	

Caretaker	12,600	
Advertising and interview expenses	1,000	
	564,520	564,520
Premises		
Repairs and maintenance	4,000	
Energy	12,000	
Water	2,200	
Rates	15,900	
Cleaning	12,400	
Grounds maintenance	2,400	
Other premises costs	1,200	
	50,100	50,100
Supplies and services		
Departmental/subject expenditure	28,000	
General office expenses	2,200	
	30,200	30,200
Contingency reserve	15,000	15,000
TOTAL		659,820

Consider what this budget format does *not* tell you. First, in this example there is no comparison with budgets of previous years. We cannot really make sense of the 1993–94 figures unless we have the equivalents for 1992–93 and preferably 1991–92. So, for example, we might have premises costs, with comparative figures, presented as:

1	2	3	4
Item	**1993–94**	**1992–93**	**1991–92**
(a) repairs and maintenance	£4,000	£5,000	£2,500
(b) energy	£12,000	£11,000	£10,000
(c) water	£2,200	£2,100	£2,000

Immediately we are better informed, and questions emerge. For example, energy expenditure has increased faster than water — why? Expenditure on repairs and maintenance has been uneven — what are the special factors here? Historical figures enable us to see trends and discrepancies, and so interrogate the budget proposal more critically.

However, sequences of historical figures do not always make for easy comparison. The problem is that the income side of the budget is not constant. It will alter according to LEA funding levels, the vagaries of the formula, changes in enrolment, inflation, etc. Also, even when the figures are conveniently rounded, as here, they are not easy to interpret. It is not immediately evident that energy is rising twice as fast as water in cash terms and with real-life figures it may be less obvious.

So, it is also important that each item should be shown as a *percentage* of the total budget for the years in question:

1 Item	5	6	7
	Percentage of total budget		
	1993–94	1992–93	1991–92
(a) repairs and maintenance	0.61	0.78	0.42
(b) energy	1.82	1.75	1.67
(c) water	0.33	0.33	0.33

Now these figures are much easier to understand, because they are limited to fewer digits and are standardised as percentages. We can see much more quickly the degree of variation in (a) and the remorseless rise of (b) as a percentage of the budget. Also (c) is now shown not to be increasing its share of the budget although it is of course increasing in cash terms.

Percentages have another virtue. They enable us to see how the budgetary cake is being sliced, and to make judgments about the relative sizes of the slices. Take the figure in the Greenglades School budget for departmental/subject expenditure, £28,000. This is revealed as 4.24% of the total budget. Does this sound reasonable? For example, how does it compare with other schools? Percentages also enable us to set parameters, eg governors could decide that departmental/subject expenditure should never be allowed to fall below a set percentage, say 3.5% of the budget.

Now these raw figures for three years, supported by their budget percentages, tell us much more than the far-too-simple original example. Yet they still do not tell us enough. An item could have a rising or constant percentage of a falling budget, which conceals the fact that less is actually spent per pupil. Both raw figures and percentages take no account of changes in pupil numbers.

Figures expressed per pupil — unit costs — take out variations of numbers to reveal the actual amount spent on each pupil, as in the following example, again for Greenglades School:

1	8	9	10
Item	Unit costs per pupil		
	1993–94	1992–93	1991–92
Departmental/subject expenditure	£63.64	£66.67	£64.19

This example shows that spending per pupil rose a little between 1991–92 and 1992–93 (3.9%) but actually declined between 1992–93 and 1993–94 *in cash terms*. In real value the decline in spending was greater, as the 1993–94 figure has less value because of inflation. So unit costs are very important for monitoring the resources actually flowing to pupils. (In this example pupil enrolment was 395, 400 and 440 for the three years respectively — the sharp rise in enrolment was not matched by a corresponding budget increase and so explains the fall in spending per pupil.)

Summing up, ideally for *budget construction* and for *evaluation at the year end*, the budget format should include, preferably over three years and certainly over two, for each item:

- projected/actual figures
- percentages of the total budget
- unit costs per pupil.

Data would have to be presented over 10 columns, not two; but in this format it provides much more useful information, and is relatively easy to use.

However, for *control and monitoring during the financial year* we only need the approved budget figure for the current year, and the actual and projected spending (and variances) to date. "Committed" expenditure can also be included. The percentage and unit cost information is not relevant for in-year monitoring.

There are two other aspects of budget presentation that need comment. One is the *degree of aggregation and disaggregation*. For example, one consolidated item, teacher salaries, is ideal for monitoring from one month to another. But for initial analysis and subsequent evaluation we need the figure disaggregated into:

- Head and deputies' salaries
- the proportion of teacher salaries allocated to administration
- discretionary spine points
- performance related pay, etc.

We need this information to enable us to understand the consolidated figure.

The second aspect is *narrative*. Often a school budget simply presents a list of figures, as in the Greenglades School example, and perhaps some appendices. At the analysis and construction stages we need a page or two of narrative:

- setting out the budget and SDP objectives
- stating how their achievement will be assessed
- possibly describing the "programmes" planned to achieve them
- describing the context of the budget (funding, enrolment, other factors, etc).

Q18. What use are unit costs?

A.   The previous question illustrated the value of unit costs for focussing on actual expenditure per pupil within a school. However, they can be put to a much wider range of uses. For example, they can be used to compare school with school, either for expenditure overall or for a specific item such as postage or electricity. Such comparisons can be very illuminating, although they raise questions rather than giving answers.

Comparisons are, of course, more likely to be valued if schools are broadly comparable in type and size (the unit costs themselves will even out the actual variations in enrolments). It is worth noting that the Audit Commission produces detailed comparative data for services such as public libraries between "peer-group" local authorities, and this has proved very useful.

Unit cost comparisons are also more valuable if they can be presented as a series over two or three years — this irons out variations and flags trends. Unit costs can also be used for comparison between LEAs, pointing out differences in funding. Current variations for comparable schools are often quite substantial between LEAs.

Unit costs are certainly not limited to "£ per pupil"; they can be expressed in any unit:

- per cubic or square metre, or hectare — useful for comparison of premises and grounds costs
- per meal or journey
- per teacher or class, or
- per unit of time — hour, day, year or teacher-hour.

There is a tendency to think of unit costs in terms of inputs — expenditure of finance and human and physical resources. But they can be expressed in terms of outcomes — the cost of a GCSE pass, at a given level, or a SAT score; or "value-added" such as the raising of a pupil's reading age. They can also be expressed in terms of process — per student-hour or class-hour. It is likely that comparative outcome and process unit costs will become more important as alternative forms of learning technology and organisation become more common, because they allow the *direct comparison* of the cost of alternatives.

Finally, there is that crucial concept of *marginal* unit costs — the additional (or reduced) cost of each student more (or less). There is a simplistic view that more students means improved funding. Clearly, each additional student brings more formula-funding, but some additional students will bring extra expenditure which far outweighs the additional funding. If a school's enrolment grows, there will be a point at which expenditure on an extra teacher, classroom, or other major item will be triggered by a particular, additional student — the last straw situation discussed in Question 36.

Unit costs are like all statistics and must be viewed with caution. They are much more complex than at first appears. For example, unit costs for, say, expenditure on fuel will be misleading, since it is largely a fixed cost and will only partially and slowly reflect changes in pupil numbers. Similarly, we would not expect unit costs on books and equipment to be comparable between an 11–16 and an 11–18 school.

> The Audit Commission publication, *Adding Up the Sums 2: Comparative Information for Schools*, is a useful source of comparative information, particularly relating to teacher salaries.

Q19. What is budget profiling?

A.   Budget profiling is the analysis of the expected patterns of expenditure and income during the financial year. For example, quarterly gas payments reflect seasonal variations:

March	£500
June	£300
September	£100
December	£400

Budget profiles are used to compare the *expected* budget position with the *actual* spending position. This will indicate whether the budget plan is on target and provide early warning of any problems.

Q20. What are the advantages of budget profiling?

A.   Budget profiling has four main advantages:

- it aids budget planning
- it provides feedback with errors and omissions when monitoring budgets
- it is a useful management tool to analyse resource consumption

- it provides important information for cash flow forecasting.

A budget profile is a prediction of the pattern of budget spending over the year. Where regular patterns or profiles can be established, they can be used as models for future plans and so reduce the amount of uncertainty in *budget planning*. Some patterns, such as seasonal fluctuations in fuel consumption, are easily identified, whereas in some areas of the budget there is no obvious pattern, eg capitation and repairs and maintenance.

The recording of budget profiles over a number of years enables comparisons to be made and provides reassurance that the budget is reasonable.

Any significant differences between the expected pattern and the actual spending position will provide *feedback* to the budget manager to highlight an area for possible concern. The difference may indicate a potential overspend or an underspend.

There may be a number of explanations for variances, including errors or omissions in budget records, or incorrect budget profiles. The reason for the variance should be investigated before any conclusion is reached.

The recording and monitoring of an expenditure profile provides information about the *pattern of consumption* over a period of time. The information can be used by managers to examine whether the consumption levels are acceptable or reasonable in comparison with different establishments, eg information may show problems such as high levels of consumption at unexpected times or overcharging.

The profile information may be used as feedback to change the practices of the organisation, for example the maximum demand of electricity sets the tariff rate, so if the demand exceeds a certain rate for a very short period the charges are made at a higher rate. Changes to consumption patterns could be made to ensure that the next tariff band is not reached and so achieve cash savings.

Cash flow forecasting uses information about expenditure and income flows to maximise cash balances and interest received. Budget profiling provides a record of spending patterns over time which may be used in the future as the basis for cash flow forecasts. This is not a significant area at the moment but could increase in importance in the future.

Q21. What are the problems associated with budget profiling?

A.   There are problems associated with using the previous year's records as a guide to profiling expenditure. For example, comparison of electricity expenditure between years may be misleading:

- records may have been incorrect, eg electricity bills incorrectly charged to the gas budget
- the meter reading may be estimated
- a new heating system may have been installed
- there may have been a particularly cold winter.

Therefore records should be compared over a number of years to gain a better picture.

Q22. What is the main aim of commitment accounting?

A.   The primary function of commitment accounting is to improve budgetary control by providing managers with a more complete and timely budget record of resources used than a financial statement of receipts and payments.

A monthly statement of receipts and payments is usually received after the end of the month and does *not* include:

- commitments made

- orders issued

- goods received but not invoiced

- invoices passed for payment.

As a budget monitoring tool such a statement is therefore not up to date. It only shows which goods and services have been paid for and does not show how much is committed and therefore how much budget is available for future use.

As soon as an order is made or a contract signed, a spending decision is taken which commits part of the budget. A commitment accounting system records a spending decision as soon as it is made rather than when the payment is made. By recording spending in this way budgets are not over-committed, ie the same allocation is not spent more than once.

Take this example which relates to the equipment budget:

	Payment record (£)	Commitment record (£)
Budget Allocation	10,000	
Ordered		3,000
Invoices paid	2,000	2,000
Balance	8,000	5,000

A monthly receipts and payments statement for equipment would show an £8000 balance, where the commitment record shows only £5000 as there is an outstanding order to the value of £3000.

Q23. How does the commitment accounting process work in practice?

A. Commitment accounting records can be kept manually or on computerised software specifically designed for schools, such as the Schools Information Management System (SIMS). The process of recording in both cases is the same.

As orders are made and recorded, the budget allocation is reduced by the estimated cost. As invoices are received, the reducing balance is amended if the actual cost is different to the estimate. This reducing balance, therefore, shows how much of the budget has not been committed and is still available to spend.

	Estimate	Adjustment	Reducing Balance
	(£)	(£)	(£)
Allocation			10,000
Computer	2,000		8,000
Lab. equipment	1,000		7,000
Table/chairs	2,000		5,000
Additional cost of lab. equip.		+200	4,800

The process relies on a correct estimate when orders are made to give a true balance. If the estimate is not reasonable, the balance will be misleading. Some budgets however, such as that for repairs, are difficult to estimate in advance as the true cost of labour and materials may not become apparent until the work has started so these records may not be accurate.

Commitments are not only made when an order is issued. Some budget lines are in effect fully committed at the beginning of the year where there is a contractual obligation such as with teaching staff salaries or cleaning contracts. This commitment means that there is no virement ability to

41

other areas unless the contract is altered. The school allocates this amount in order to meet the staffing and cleaning contract commitments for the full financial year.

For services such as electricity, gas and water, where no orders are made, the initial budget allocation is a commitment for a certain level of consumption, normally based on the previous years' consumption levels.

Q24. **What are the best methods for allocating funds to internal budget-holders?**

A.   Allocating funds to internal budget-holders has always been a problem, even when funds were limited to the old capitation allowance. There are actually three aspects to the problem.

1. *Deciding what proportion of the total budget should be delegated.* There is a temptation for the central budget holder — usually the Head — to hold funds back, perhaps for "central funds", or a "contingency fund". Often this is for legitimate whole-school planning, but sometimes it can be due to a reluctance to let go and an expression of "school management knows best". This is in conflict with the spirit of LMS, namely maximum delegation to the lowest level. There may be a case for such central funds, but these should not be a rationalisation for avoiding full delegation!

2. *Deciding how the portion of the school budget to be delegated should actually be allocated.* First, it may be helpful to distinguish between "maintenance" and "development", since different approaches are needed. There are four strategies commonly used.

- *Benevolent despotism* — the Head, or sometimes deputy Head or bursar, decides, with varying degrees of consultation. Despotism can be incisive, purposeful and time-saving. On the other hand it can also be affected by the personal preferences and prejudices of the despot.

- *Open market* — all the staff (in a primary school) or a finance/heads of department committee (in a secondary or larger primary school) adjudicates on bids for funds. Open market is more democratic and consensual, and involves greater staff consultation. But it takes more time, and may give pushy claimants preference over modest ones. Currently it is often used for allocating "development" funds and also for deciding on any formula for formula allocation.

- *Incrementalism* — updating last year's figures for changes in formula funding and perhaps other changes. Incrementalism is difficult to defend, but it is based on the bedrock of last year's spending; and it is time-saving. It is probably more common than schools like to admit.

- *Formula allocation* — usually based upon some allowance for numbers of pupils or "pupil-periods", adjusted by a weighting for the costliness of the activity. Formula allocation is more open and appears to be fairer. It is time-saving once it is set up, and can be projected for future years. However the construction of the formula is still a difficult and subjective process.

The problem can also be analysed in a different way. Tim Simkins (see below) has suggested that there are four different dimensions which schools should consider in allocating funds.

- How is information on previous spending and on proposed needs collected? How are proposals set out, justified and prioritised?

- How full and open are the discussions and the consultations about allocation?

43

- What criteria are used, eg experience of previous years (incrementalism), qualitative judgment, linking to objectives or formula?
- Who should be responsible for the ultimate decisions, and how should these be made?

3. *Deciding what mechanism should be used to distribute the funds which have been allocated to budget-holders.* Often once funds have been allocated they are made available to budget holders as a straight "gift without strings", ie the right to spend up to the given limit. But there are at least 13 other mechanisms which can be used, eg earmarked funds (funds tied to a particular purpose), matching funds ("I'll give you half if you find the rest") or funds related to specific outcomes, or within a pool ("£X is available for fieldwork expenses, first come first served").

The issues above are discussed more fully in Knight B, *Financial Management for Schools: The Thinking Manager's Guide* (1993, Heinemann Education), pp. 60–75; Simkins T, "Patronage, Markets and Collegiality: Reflections on the Allocation of Finance in Secondary Schools" in *Education Management and Administration*, 14(1) pp. 17–30; and Boulton A, "A Developed Formula for the Distribution of Capitation Allowances" in *Educational Management and Administration*, 14(1) pp.31–38.

Q25. How can the financial needs of the curricular or other areas be assessed?

A.   The requirement here is to make an objective assessment of needs by clarifying, quantifying and, if possible, prioritising them.

The Publishers' Association has produced a simple tool which was designed to assess textbook and similar learning resource needs, but can be used to assess needs of any kind. It comprises an empty matrix proforma, the *Learning Resources Assessor* (LRA), which can be adapted to fit the situation of any school.

A single matrix sheet could be used for each class teacher in a primary school, with a line for each curriculum area and a column for each type of resource. Alternatively, a sheet could be used for each subject area in a secondary school, with a line for each year group and columns for each type of resource. In fact the proforma can be used for any area of need in a school.

The separate sheets are filled in using a 1–5 assessment scale (1 = high need, 5 = low need) against a set of single criteria which are provided, eg:

1 = unacceptable situation. Poor supply of essential re- sources, with extensive sharing, and/or in poor condition. Few additional desirable resources available

2 = mediocre situation…, and so on.

The completed sheets can then be collated and areas which have a high concentration of assessment scores 1 and 2 can then be identified easily.

The *Learning Resources Assessor* is set out in *How to Assess Your School's Book Needs* (1991), from the Publishers' Association, 19 Bedford Square, London WC1B 3HT.

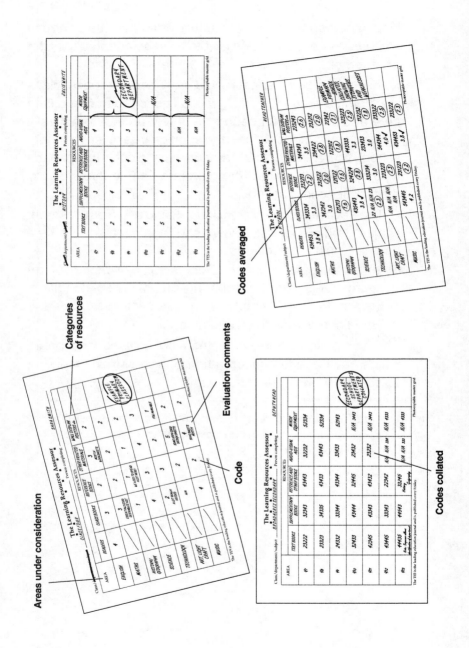

Areas under consideration

Categories of resources

Evaluation comments

Code

Codes averaged

Codes collated

Q26. How should non-public funds be dealt with?

A.   Most schools have funds at their disposal which come from neither central government nor the LEA.

Parent/teacher associations, friends of the school, private donations from companies or individuals, fund-raising events and activities are all sources of extra funding for schools. Such funds, though not public money, nevertheless need accounting for with the same care and efficiency.

These unofficial school funds may be handed over to the school for particular purposes, eg for special equipment, for the provision of a careers suite, for specific school journeys, etc. Individuals and organisations donating or raising money for particular purposes are entitled to know that the money was spent correctly. Therefore, separate accounts should be kept and audited financial statements produced.

Procedures should be in place, with the usual safeguards as to chequebooks and signatures, similar to those used to deal with public funding.

Regular reports on the state of the accounts should be made to finance committees, governing bodies and the annual meeting of parents.

Q27. Who is responsible for arranging insurance cover?

A.   The LEA will normally issue schools with an insurance manual or an advice document in which details of all insurance cover taken out by the LEA is listed. If no such manual has been issued then ask the LEA for details.

Policies should include:

- employers' liability
- fire
- libel and slander

- motor insurance
- personal accident
- public liability
- school journeys, etc.

Many of these policies have been extended to include cover for governors.

The LEA financial statement required under s.42 of the Education Reform Act 1988 (see Question 6) gives some indication of the size of the expenditure on insurance premiums. For example, in 1993/94, one LEA allowed for expenditure amounting to £730,000 on insurance premiums, 26% of which is allocated to governor insurance to cover potential liability in negligence towards staff or third parties incurred in the exercise of governors' responsibilities.

Since the introduction of LMS and delegated budgets many LEAs have examined the insurance cover previously held and decided that expenditure for some insurance should be delegated to schools. Some LEAs have decided to discontinue some policies because of the practical difficulties involved or the cost of premiums.

Insurance covering vandalism and theft, or accidental damage, has been dropped by some LEAs with schools offered the option of:

- taking out blanket cover for all contents
- taking out cover for specific items such as computers and videos
- not to insure at all and meet the cost of all losses from the school budget.

The risk factor will vary from school to school with some suffering vandalism on a large scale and others with few or no occurrences. Theft is another matter, with most schools having some incidents and a large number experiencing the loss of many valuable items. Therefore, two things are of utmost importance: good security arrangements and adequate insurance.

Insurance companies will insist on certain minimum security precautions, such as identification marks, the locking away of some items, etc. Some schools have installed video cameras whilst others employ security firms to visit the school site several times each day out of school hours.

A GM school should cover all risks required by the DFE and receives a sum in its special purpose grant to cover 50% of the cost of premises insurance to a maximum of £6000. Other insurance cover must be met from the school budget.

Q28. How can staff absence through injury or sickness be covered?

A. Most LEAs organise a scheme to cover staff absence through injury and/or sickness. The scheme is usually arranged to come into effect after a specified number of days' absence, eg immediately or after 3, 6, 10, 19 days, etc.

In the first three years of LMS, until the insurance companies learned of the risks by experience, premiums were low and claims were high. Several companies paid dearly for the experience and some even went out of business dealing with this type of insurance. The situation now is quite different with many schools opting for the highest number of days before a claim can be made in order to keep the cost of premiums down.

Some schools have taken a conscious decision to take up no insurance cover for staff who are absent due to injury or sickness. They either rely on the goodwill of staff to cover absent colleagues or meet the cost from the school budget share. In conclusion, schools will need to assess their own risk factor and weigh this up against the cost of premiums.

Insurance Guide for Schools

1. Ascertain what insurance cover is provided by the LEA or controlling body.

2. Consider what risks are not covered by the LEA or voluntary body which it is necessary to cover.

3. Take advice from the LEA's insurance department a reputable broker.

4. Consider taking out cover for specific items on loan and ensure that expensive items temporarily removed from school are covered, eg musical instruments. Some "all risks policies" state that such items are covered automatically.

5. Obtain letters of indemnity from parents of pupils undertaking schools trips or visits. Accidents to pupils on trips in recent years have made parents, schools and LEAs more aware of the need for adequate insurance cover. LEAs have issued codes of practice and these should be followed to the letter. (It should be pointed out to parents that the local authority's insurance cover is limited to the legal responsibilities arising from negligence. Parents should be made aware of the insurance cover that has been arranged so that they can take out additional cover if they so wish.)

6. Notify the insurers, LEA or voluntary body of any new risks, property, equipment or vehicles which need to be added to the cover already provided; or take out the necessary cover.

---

7. Inform the insurers, LEA or voluntary body of any loss, accident or incident which may give rise to an insurance claim.

8. Avoid giving indemnity to any third party without first obtaining the approval of the insurers, LEA or voluntary body.

9. Carry out an annual review of the total insurance cover carried and make decisions about updating to avoid under or over insurance in all areas. An OFSTED inspection team will need to be assured that such an annual review is undertaken.

FACTORS AFFECTING THE BUDGET

Q29.   How can an inadequate allowance for inflation be identified?

A.   It is important to be clear about what inflation is. It is *not* increased costs — though it may contribute to them — because these also can be created by improvements in quality (eg a fall in the pupil-teacher ratio (PTR)), increases in volume (eg more pupils or longer school day/year), or a change in the "factors of production" (eg more use of computer technology). *Inflation is an increase in the prices of a given quantity and mix of goods of the same quality —* often called a "basket" of goods and services. Most LEAs have their own educational basket of goods, against which they assess inflation.

The first step is to assess inflation as it affects the school budget. You could use the figure your LEA has derived from its own basket but these figures vary a good deal in validity from LEA to LEA. You could use the retail price index (RPI), but this measures a different set of goods and services (including mortgage charges) than those used in a school. The best guide available is the Treasury gross domestic product (GDP) deflator used by the Government. This omits mortgage interest and import price changes, although it is not, of course, specifically calculated for educational salaries, goods and services. You may wish to make specific allowance for mandatory awards relating to teachers' pay since this will be by far the largest single inflationary factor.

Once you have established your best estimate of inflation, you can check this against funding in your LEA, either by looking at the budget increase of schools who have had no change in age weighted pupil units (AWPU) or other formula elements, or by calculating the formula funding which your school would have received in the current year if its AWPU had not altered.

> How to obtain and use the GDP deflator is set out in Knight B, *Financial Management for Schools: The Thinking Manager's Guide* (1993, Heinemann Education), pp.102–3.

Q30. What is the effect of an inadequate allowance for inflation?

A.   An insufficient supplement in funding to counter inflation is serious for a number of reasons.

- It amounts to a cut in real terms, ie in the purchasing power of a given amount of money. So it has exactly the same effects as an overt cut in funds (see Question 8). The school will normally alter its budget to protect some areas of expenditure, so concentrating the effect on others. These will often be just those areas when the effect lingers on for several years.

- Unless there is a positive attempt to restore this underfunding, the effect of an under-allowance for inflation goes on and is compounded year on year.

- Each year that the shortfall is uncorrected, the more difficult it is to rectify. A 1% underfunding in year 1 needs almost a 5% correction by year 5. Even this would only correct year 5 expenditure — it would not undo the damage in years 1–4.

Q31. Is it desirable to carry forward a surplus at the end of the financial year?

A.   A large number of schools do carry forward a surplus, sometimes a large one, and often from year to year, par-

ticularly in the early years of managing their delegated budget. Schools tend to put forward a range of justifications:
- caution in an unfamiliar situation
- protection against the unexpected
- accumulation for further projects, and
- failure of invoices from the current year to be charged to that year's budget. (Sometimes it is argued that much of the surplus was *committed* in the financial year but that the invoices were only paid after it. This is not a good argument, since although there will actually be a charge in the following year this is likely to be offset by another carry-over of similar commitments at that year's end — see Question 22 for an explanation of *commitment accounting.*)

This appearance of a surplus is very understandable in the first year or two of LMS, but it is difficult to defend as a regular practice because:
- it suggests poor planning and budget construction if the surplus has "just grown"
- it is damaging politically since it takes away any possibility of the school suggesting that it needs more funds
- it would lose value in real terms unless it can be invested at a rate at least as high as the current rate of inflation.

It would be much more acceptable if a surplus was deliberately planned and assigned for a specific purpose, eg:
- a major specified project
- a capital replacement fund
- a contingency fund (but this too is open to criticism, see the next question).

GM schools are allowed to carry over 2.5% of their annual maintenance grant for general purposes, and a further 10%

for premises and capital expenditure. This seems a sensible arrangement.

Q32. Is it desirable to create a contingency fund?

A.   Most LEAs advised LMS schools to make provision in their budgets for contingencies. However, there are quite strong arguments against this practice.

- A small contingency fund — say 0.5% of the budget, or less — is of little value. Contingencies below this level can often be met within the swings and roundabouts of the budgetary year, or could be carried forward without seriously affecting the following year's budget.

- A contingency fund larger than say 0.5% is tying up too much money for an eventuality which will only rarely occur.

- Most items of the school budget should be predicted with reasonable accuracy. The most unpredictable area is the teacher salaries budget, which is affected by teacher movement and by changes in enrolment which affect the school's organisation by classes (see Question 36). Here, however, the fact that the school and financial year do not coincide works to the schools' advantage, since any adverse change in enrolment will occur in September and so only affect $7/12$ (September to March) of the financial year.

- Some schools come to use the contingency fund as a kind of nest-egg for the year end, and so tend to spend it for immediate priorities then — rather than the priorities planned for at the start of the year.

There is one strong argument for contingency funds. Schools currently work in a very turbulent environment, where it is very difficult to plan from one year to another and where cuts in funding or changes in government demands can fall from a clear sky. So some kind of permanent financial cushion does have a strong attraction.

A good solution is to transfer any existing contingency fund or surplus carried forward, or at least part of it, to start up a capital replacement fund which is then topped up each year (see Question 45). This would normally be drawn upon each year for capital replacement but would always be available as a cushion if a desperate situation developed.

Q33. What are the fixed costs of a school?

A. In theory, at least, fixed costs are easily defined. *Fixed costs* are those costs which do not alter when the number of pupils enrolled alters — in economists' jargon, when the "volume of economic activity" alters. So the costs are fixed in this precise technical sense. Of course they are not fixed in a normal household sense as they still move up or down as suppliers alter their prices. So, for example, telephone rental is a totally fixed charge — it is not affected by any change in pupil enrolment — but the annual charge can still go up or down at the behest of the operator. Fixed costs can vary for other reasons. A building may need additional repairs, but the cost is still technically fixed because the extra charge *has not been caused by changes in pupil numbers*. Rental fixed costs, of course, are not unalterable; a school can alter its telephone rental by changing the equipment.

Although fixed costs are easily defined they are not so easily identified. This is because there are few items in a school budget which are *totally fixed* — such as telephone rental — or *totally variable*. In fact the only totally variable cost is probably the cost of ingredients for school meals —

not normally included within LMS budgets. It could be expected that classroom stationery would be very closely related to pupil numbers, but even here a proportion will be fixed, like paper for wall display.

Almost all items in the budget lie along a spectrum from "mainly fixed" to "mainly variable". A good example of *mainly fixed costs* could be the Head's salary. Changes in this will not be triggered automatically by a rise in pupil numbers unless governors choose to use their discretion. If numbers fall the Head's salary will not normally fall. Other mainly fixed costs include:

- deputy heads' salaries
- discretionary spine points (unless awarded for a limited term)
- support staff salaries
- energy costs
- building repairs and maintenance
- cleaning
- grounds maintenance
- furniture and fittings.

At the other end of the spectrum, *mainly variable costs* include items affected by the size of the teacher establishment:

- basic teacher salaries
- teacher support salaries
- advertising and other establishment expenses, and INSET
- water, if metered
- books, stationery and materials
- insurance and other services with charges relating to pupil numbers.

While it is difficult to define specific expenditure items as simply fixed or variable, it is possible to estimate for each item the *proportion* which is fixed, and by aggregating these to estimate the overall fixed proportion of the budget. This has been estimated at 20–30% for most schools when they are at full capacity (more when they are significantly under-capacity, see the next question).

There is a second element of confusion. The definition of fixed/variable depends on our time horizon. What is fixed this year may become variable in years to come. Take that very fixed item, telephone rental. If a school's numbers fall heavily, the school might decide — perhaps after several years — to reduce its telephone system. At that point telephone rental is a variable cost — although once it has altered it becomes fixed again. Obviously the longer this time horizon, the more scope the school has for varying fixed charges, and so the smaller the proportion of fixed costs. So, for example, a heavy fall in enrolment might lead to a sell-off or mothballing of premises, and so a reduction in a whole range of premises-related costs with quite a high fixed element.

An interesting example of the effect of time horizons occurs with examination fees in secondary schools. These are totally variable, ie related to student numbers, but only after a lag of several years during which period they are totally fixed! This is because a reduction in intake numbers in, say, an 11–16 school will not affect examination costs until the year 7 cohort reaches year 11, four years later.

Fixed costs are not as easy to identify as one might think but they are still a very important concept for school financial management.

Q34. How does falling pupil enrolment affect a school's budget?

A. When a school's enrolment falls, its costs for maintaining the same level of educational provision do not fall *in proportion*. This is because the fixed cost element of the budget, usually around 20–30% when the school is at full capacity, does not alter and so becomes a larger proportion of the budget. This in turn creates an increase in expenditure per pupil, which we can call the *fixed cost excess* (FCE) — see the diagram below.

A model of school costs

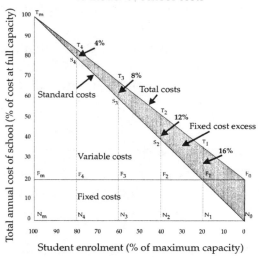

Reproduced from: Knight B, *Financial Management for Schools: The Thinking Manager's Guide*, p.109 (Heinemann Education).

A school's costs would fall along the line T_m–N_0 if there were no fixed costs. In this case unit costs per pupil would remain constant whatever the size of the school. However, the fixed cost — shown here as a conservative 20% of the school's total annual costs at full capacity, below the line F_m–F_o, only allow costs to fall along the line T_m–F_o. The difference between these fall lines is the FCE — the additional expenditure required as numbers fall to maintain the same level of provision.

The lower enrolment falls, the greater the FCE. What is less obvious is that it also becomes *proportionately* greater. For example, at 80% enrolment the FCE will require an additional 4% of the school's original costs at full capacity on top of a reduced 80% budget; at 60% enrolment the FCE will be an extra 8% on a 60% budget; at 40%, 12% on a 40% budget; and so on. So the FCE creates an exponential rise in unit costs per pupil.

It is possible to calculate the FCE mathematically. For example, a school with a budget of £1,000,000 falling from full to 60% enrolment will require an FCE of

$$\frac{8}{68} \times £1,000,000 = £117,647$$

to maintain the same level of provision.

The fixed cost excess is not just a useful concept; it is a mathematical certainty. It cannot be avoided if school enrolment falls, and has to be paid.

Q.35 Who pays the fixed cost excess (FCE)?

A.   This will depend on the school's funding arrangements. At independent schools parents will pay for the FCE in increased fees, unless the school can reduce the level of provision or make itself more efficient. In LEA schools the LEA will pay a proportion of the FCE (perhaps approximately half to two-thirds) through those parts of its formula which are not pupil-related; and the school will pay the rest. But even the LEA share of the FCE will actually be paid by other schools, since it will not be available for delegation to them.

> For a fuller explanation of fixed costs and the FCE, see Knight B, *Financial Management for Schools: The Thinking Manager's Guide* (1993, Heinemann Education), chapter six.

Q36. How do decisions about pupil grouping affect the budget?

A.   Dramatically! In fact although it is often said that the curriculum determines the budget, this is not true. It is the organisation of pupils into classes that largely determines the budget, through its direct effect upon the teaching establishment.

Suppose a secondary school has 150 pupils in year 7 and it decides to create five classes. But if it now has 151..., 152..., 153..., 160..., 165... at what point does it decide to break the year-group into six classes? At the point of creating an additional class an additional £20,000 (say) in salary and on-costs is incurred. This *breaking point* is a subjective one, and depends on the funding, culture, history and environment of the school. In every secondary school it exists for every year-group — the enrolment point at which another class is created. In the worst scenario an 11–16 school could find itself with each of the five year-groups just over the breaking point — and so with five extra classes.

In primary schools, the situation is a little more flexible since the school may decide to provide mixed-age classes. In this case the school can be treated as a continuous sequence of classes with only one overall breaking point. Nevertheless, in an average school with 200–300 pupils or so, the effect can still be substantial, as the boxed example shows.

The effects of pupil grouping on the budget

Suppose a primary school with 270 pupils is at present divided into 10 classes. What happens if it reduces to nine or even eight classes?

(a) 270 pupils in 10 classes means classes of average size 27
(b) 270 pupils in nine classes means classes of average size 30
(c) 270 pupils in eight classes means classes of average size 33/34.

Now (b) will save the school (say) £20,000 on a budget of perhaps £350,000, ie nearly 6% of the total. Option (c) would save (say) £40,000, or 11% of the budget.

So, are the disadvantages in terms of increased class size of options (b) or (c) for one year, or more, worth the financial gain, and what it will buy? Conversely, is the opportunity cost of option (a) over option (b) of £20,000 pa worth the gains in pupil achievement and outcomes for a class size reduction from 30 to 27?

BUDGET MONITORING, CONTROL AND EVALUATION

Q37. How should budget variances be analysed and treated?

A. Budget variances will usually be shown on a printout which compares actual with expected expenditure for a particular stage of the year. (Better systems profile the "expected" figures to reflect seasonal patterns of spending.) Your response to the printout variance will obviously depend on its size — particularly if it is an over-spend! But you need to decide what *kind* of variance it is; there are four possibilities. The variance could be:

- *an error*
- *an oscillation* — a variation in expenditure, perhaps caused by delays or bunching of invoices, or by variation in ordering patterns
- *a one-off event* — some unexpected change or reduction which is not likely to be repeated
- *a trend* — an increase or decrease in expenditure from the anticipated level which is likely to continue and which can be projected.

Obviously an error can be corrected, and an oscillation ignored. But what about the substantive variances, whether one-off or extended into a trend?

The first question to ask is whether the variances arise from changes in *price* or changes in *volume*. If the former, then the cause of the variance is beyond your control. All you can do is to see whether you can economise on the item in some way, to reduce expenditure to the original expected level; and if not, to look for economies elsewhere in the budget to offset it (see the boxed example below).

Example of quarterly telephone expenditure

Date	Expected to date (£)	Actual to date (£)	Variance (£)
June	300	400	100
September	600	800	200
December	900	1150	250
March	1200	1500	300

Assuming you can check the actual bills, and there is no reason to think they are incorrect, then these variances are not errors. For June you might consider the variance is an oscillation. By September this looks much less likely, and you find that prices have risen more than expected, but also that the volume of calls is greater than projected. An economy campaign is launched — so the trend in December and March is reduced but not removed. Meanwhile savings have been identified elsewhere which offset the accumulated March variance.

See Redmond T, "Micawber Rules OK" in *School Governor* September 1990, pp. 10–13.

Q38. What is needed for effective financial control?

A.   The terms "control" and "monitoring" are sometimes used synonymously, but in fact they are quite different. *Control* requires setting up systems to ensure that money is spent for the purposes for which it has been authorised, and that proper standards have been adopted for the school's financial management. *Monitoring* involves the process discussed in Question 37, namely checking whether actual expenditure tallies with the pattern expected, and whether any remedial action is needed. (Monitoring may, of course, also uncover issues which have control implications.)

Recent publications by the Audit Commission (see below) have produced useful guidance for schools. They suggest a set of standards in the following areas:

- organisation of responsibility and accountability — definition of roles, limits of delegated authority, register of financial interests
- budget management, particularly objectives, securing value for money, and effective monitoring
- internal controls — a system of checks, written procedures, provision for staff absence, sound records, traceability of transactions
- insurance — adequacy, annual review
- computer system — effective back-up — disaster recovery plan, controlled access, registration under the Data Protection Act 1984
- purchasing — value for money, provision for quotations and tenders, ordering procedures, checking and authorisation of payments
- personnel — personnel procedures, records, processing and checking payroll transactions
- assets — security of cash, capital assets and stock, maintenance and checking of inventories, procedures for borrowing items
- income — charging policy, collection and receipts from income, reconciliation with bank records, bad debts
- banking arrangements — definition of limits, signatories, cheque procedures, reconciliation of bank records, investment of surplus funds
- petty cash — agreed level, procedures, checks
- voluntary funds (to the same standards as the school's public funds) — treasurer and auditor, procedures, signatories, annual accounts, insurance/fidelity arrangements, separation from official funds.

The joint Audit Commission/OFSTED publication, *Keeping your Balance*, sets out standards for financial administration in schools, while the Audit Commission's *Adding Up the Sums: Schools' Management of their Finance* (1993, HMSO), describes the current situation in schools. The Rainbow Pack for GM schools contains valuable guidance.

A useful user-friendly article is Goodman D, "Sharks and Sharp Practice" in *School Governor*, November 1990.

Q39. How important is inventory control?

A.   Stocktaking is a chore in any organisation, so keeping proper stock of the school's assets and checking their existence annually will not be a popular activity. However, it is important. Legally, the Head and governing body are responsible for the proper care and protection of the assets entrusted to their care. Practically, efficient stocktaking holds stock holders accountable, reduces loss and the likelihood of resources being unused or duplicated, and so ultimately makes better value of the school's financial resources. Also, a good inventory is essential for cases of fire or substantial theft.

The foundation for inventory control is an effective inventory system. Two types of inventories are required: one for large and durable items (equipment, furniture, fittings, etc) and one for minor items (books, small items of equipment, audio-visual aids, computer software,etc). The former will comprise capital items which need assessment of depreciation (see Question 43); the latter day-to-day items which will not be consumed within the year, in the way that stationery and materials are (see the boxed example).

Each inventory needs a column to show:

(a) the name of the item

(b) the number of units allocated at the start of the inventory (stock at start)

(c) the actual number of units found by stocktaking (stock at present)

(d) the discrepancy betwen (b) and (c) (variation) with a code for explanation and the initials of the person responsible.

Columns (c) and (d) appear for each year and additional purchases can also be added.

Example of an inventory for day-to-day items

	1990–91			1991–92		
Item	Stock at start	Stock at present	Variation	Stock at start	Stock at present	Variation
Writing	54	50	4 [2 WO]	50	40	10 [2 WO]
English			[1 M]			[6 M]
Book 1			[1 T]			[2 T]

WO = written off

M = missing

T = transferred to

An inventory system needs to be managed properly. New acquisitions must be entered up systematically. After stock-taking, probably at the end of the academic year, each budget-holder should provide a summary sheet showing the numbers of "written off" and "missing" items. All major losses will need investigation.

Q40. How should a school evaluate its budget out-turn?

A.   Probably in most schools evaluation of the budget is the least effective part of the budget process. The reasons for this are partly technical — by the time the final out-turn statement appears the new financial year has probably been under way for two or more months and the urgency for budget evaluation has receded — and partly methodo-logical. It is not always clear what should be evaluated, or how this can best be done.

Budgetary evaluation is best divided into two parts:

- *immediate evaluation* of the budget and resource man-agement, as soon as possible after the final out-turn statement, and
- *longer-term evaluation*, focusing on the educational out-comes of the budget.

The immediate evaluation is much more straightforward. Here you need to ascertain or assess:

- the final surplus or deficit, and the main reasons for it
- underspends or overspends for particular items, and the reasons for these
- any trends developing
- any problems in the budget process itself, eg budget reporting, monitoring and corrective action
- financial information — its accuracy, promptness and also the effectiveness of presentation (see Question 17)
- comparison by headings with the out-turns of previous year(s), with an adjustment for inflation
- comparisons with other schools, where figures are known and comparable
- scope for further savings or greater efficiency.

You should also be interested in the efficient use of re-sources and aim for:

- value for money in purchase of supplies and services
- effectiveness of contracts
- efficient use and maintenance of premises
- efficient deployment of support staff
- efficient deployment of teachers and optimum contact ratios
- effectiveness of allowances, performance-related payments and fringe benefits.

Longer-term evaluation is much more difficult. The budget may have specific objectives, perhaps linked to the SDP, but actual assessment of the extent to which they have been achieved may be difficult and may not be possible at the end of the financial year. But the budget may also have other unstated but implied objectives, eg to fund the school's "normal" educational programme — and relating achievements here to the budget certainly can be difficult.

Two practical possibilities suggest themselves. First, did the budget have explicit objectives, eg "to improve the school environment"? If so:

- can you assess this achievement, qualitatively or quantitatively? In some cases there will have been informal or formal evaluation. But even in others you can at least make some sort of judgment
- does the expenditure related to this objective look like a sensible return on your investment?
- were the "right" amount of resources allocated to it? Or too few? Or too many?
- could you have achieved the same or better results by different means?

Second, we can ask whether any features of the school have been recently evaluated, formally or informally, or whether any are about to be. If so, we can take this evaluation and add a financial dimension.

- Does this feature look like a reasonable return on the finance devoted to it?
- Did you allocate the right amount of resources to it?
- Could a greater or smaller allocation have been more cost-efficient?
- Could you have achieved the same results by different means?

The key to this long-term evaluation lies in basing it not on the budget but on *existing educational evaluation* within the school, as and when it occurs. It would be foolish to set up a separate evaluation of outcomes just for the budget; it makes more sense to wait until the evaluation arises naturally, and then link it to the budget. But there is one *caveat.* You must concentrate on *pupil outcomes*, not on the school process.

Suppose, for example, that a primary school gives priority in the budget to improving science, then the evaluation must focus not on science classes, teaching or the curriculum, but on pupils' understanding, knowledge and skills in science. It is the progress in this area that would need to be matched against the additional expenditure.

Q41. What is the distinction between cost-efficiency and cost-effectiveness?

A. The two terms are often used interchangeably and although there is some overlap — one affecting the other — they should be used with care.

Efficiency is a high level of attainment of specific standards or objectives, eg a heating system which consistently heats classrooms to the desired temperature, or a report system which provides parents with detailed and helpful information on their children at regular and stated intervals.

Cost-efficiency relates the concept of efficiency to cost. So a high level of cost-efficiency implies high efficiency and low costs. The two are related, since the lower the cost the lower the level of efficiency that might be acceptable, and vice versa. For example, a heating system may be efficient but if the boiler is gobbling fuel at an astronomical cost, it is certainly *not* cost-efficient. Replacing the boiler with a more economical one may make no difference to the heating efficiency of the classrooms, but it will certainly increase cost-efficiency.

Effectiveness in the school context means a high level of achievement of the school's objectives. So high examination or assessment scores, high pupil attendance, good standards of pupil behaviour, close interaction with the local community, would all be examples of effectiveness. (Note that they need to be relative to the quality of pupil intake and the local catchment area.)

Cost-effectiveness again relates the concept of effectiveness to cost. For example, a physical education programme with an objective to teach all pupils to swim 50 metres and which succeeds in doing so can be rated as 100% effective. However, if this is only achieved by devoting a high proportion of the teacher's time to this activity, to the great disadvantage of others, it is *not* cost-effective.

The terms are not always clearly distinct. It is not always easy or perhaps profitable to decide which activity best fits each term. There are certainly borderline examples — and efficiency affects effectiveness. A more efficient heating system should improve the classroom environment and so pupil learning; more efficient registration should reduce truancy and lead to improved outcomes, etc. Similarly, improved cost-efficiency will, other things being equal, improve cost-effectiveness.

Between the two concepts lie two others "value for money" and "productivity". *Value for money* is focused on the *choice* of supplies and services, to improve mainly cost-efficiency. *Productivity* is focused on the *organisation* of the school's resources, to improve cost-effectiveness.

For an academic study of cost-effectiveness in 16+ education, see Thomas H, *Education Costs and Performance: A Cost Effectiveness Analysis* (1990, Cassell).

CAPITAL REPLACEMENT AND COSTING

Q42. What is the distinction between "capital" and "revenue"?

A.   Capital expenditure is usually classified as major durable items, such as buildings and land, and large items of equipment such as a lathe or a piano. Also, major projects to build and equip a new building, or a major renovation programme, will involve a capital expenditure element.

Normally, capital expenditures are seen as separate from the annual revenue budget because they are large, one-off expenditures which distort the annual revenue budget picture, and which bring into one year expenditure which should really be regarded as spread over the life of the items. If items are paid by a loan or leased, then the loan or leasing charges obviously appear in the budget. (While leasing is a popular device in the private sector, because it is often tax-efficient there, it is often not worthwhile in state schools because of high interest and administrative costs.)

However, the distinction between capital and revenue is not black and white. Uncertainty arises in three ways.

- *The matter of degree* — at what point is an item classified as "major and durable"? A pair of scissors would definitely not qualify while a piano would easily; but what about a microscope?

- *The source of funding* — capital items of the smaller kind may still be funded from the revenue budget (technically called "revenue contributions towards capital outlay", and this may even apply to building improvements).

- *The question of replacement* — often items which were originally regarded as capital will be replaced by expenditure from the annual budget; furniture is usually re-placed in this way, and even large items like a piano.

The distinction between capital and revenue is not neces-sarily an important one for budgetary purposes. However, the *concept* of capital items is very important — because it leads to the idea of an item being bought in year 1 but being consumed over years 1–[N], and so to ideas of depreciation and planned capital replacement.

Q43. How should allowance be made for depreciation?

A.   State schools have never really allowed for depreciation. They just used equipment until it wore out and then peti-tioned the LEA to replace it. Now under LMS they need to provide equipment for themselves.

Depreciation is an accountant's concept of the decline of an asset over time. An item which lasts for 10 years may be thought of as having one-tenth of its value consumed each year, so we need to write off some of the book value each year. However, this can only occur on a balance sheet, since it relates to *consumption* (not in the annual budget) — and *not to expenditure*. The actual expenditure for the asset will only show up once in the budget at the time of the initial purchase (unless it is leased or bought with a loan paid back over a longer period).

Therefore, allowing for depreciation on the balance sheet does not actually set aside any money to offset it. For this you need a *capital replacement fund*, fed from annual transfers from the budget.

Q44. How can the size of a capital replacement fund be calculated?

A.   This is done quite easily as follows:

- Take your inventory of capital equipment and similar assets.
- Remove as many of the smaller items as you can — these you can reasonably assume will be replaced from internal budget-holders' funds.
- For each remaining asset, divide its current replacement cost by the number of years of life left to give its *annual replacement cost.*
  Total the annual replacement costs for all the items — this gives you the amount you need to feed into the capital replacement fund this year.
- For the next year, simply update for inflation and add the annual replacement costs of any items purchased since your original assessment.

This process is repeated each year.

Of course it is likely that you will not be able to afford the amount needed to finance the replacement fund! If so, you have at least identified a *capital replacement gap*, which can then be notified to the governors, the LEA, your MP and anyone else who will listen!

A capital replacement fund is also a more acceptable form of carrying forward a surplus — see Question 31.

Calculating the annual replacement cost

Asset (a)	Current replacement cost (b)	Estimated years of life remaining (c)	Annual replacement cost (b/c)
Computer	£1,000	5	£200

An actual example of a proforma to assess capital replacement needs is given in Knight B, *Financial Management for Schools: The Thinking Manager's Guide* (1993, Heinemann Education), page 116.

Q45. How can capital replacement be financed?

A.   The best method is a capital replacement fund, topped up each year as suggested above (Question 44). This assesses the need systematically and can be drawn on as required. It also evens out peaks and troughs of replacement expenditure. However, it is important that the fund can be invested with a rate of interest *at least equal to the current rate of inflation*. Otherwise it will decline in real purchasing value.

Another source for a capital replacement fund for many schools may be a surplus carried forward. Many schools are regularly rolling forward surpluses and it makes sense to use at least part of these amounts to start such a fund. Similarly, contingency funds could be switched into the replacement fund, particularly as the arguments for keeping these are weak (see Question 32). The capital replacement fund could still be available as a back-up to meet really extreme contingencies.

If any of the above are impracticable it may be possible to take out a loan. At times of inflation this makes good sense, since inflation favours debtors, and the annual cost of repayments shrinks *in real terms* over time.

But only a few LEAs make loans to schools, though others may allow schools to spend beyond their budget allocation for a specific agreed purpose.

For GM Schools the Rainbow Pack prohibits borrowing or overdrafts. However, in the longer term it would be logical for self-managing schools to borrow, like private schools or other businessses — but caution would be needed!

Q46. How should a major project be costed?

A.   There are some important principles to follow.

- Be sure that the objectives of the project are clear. You can then check that all the project requirements are really necessary — or even if the project is actually worthwhile.
- Identify *all* costs. Be alert for any ongoing commitments you may be incurring, eg for additional staffing, security, insurance, maintenance and replacement. Look out for hidden extras, eg additional power points needed for new equipment.
- Include non-financial costs, eg wear and tear, use of premises, time, and even the intangibles such as health and morale. Some of these can be given a cash equivalent, eg two hours robbed from secretarial support has a value elsewhere. If you cannot give them a cash equivalent, just log them up in words.

- Identify the potential realistic benefits, again both financial and non-financial. You can then assess if the benefits are worth the costs — a crude form of cost-benefit analysis.

- Distinguish between start-up costs — which may be spread over more than one year — and steady-state costs. (Start-up costs are those involved in setting up the project from scratch. Steady-state costs are those incurred from maintaining and running the project once it has been set up.) You need a budget for the start-up year(s) and one for the steady-state situation (keep to current, this year, prices, to allow comparisons). Remember to allow for replacement of equipment and that some costs may rise in future years, such as salary increments.

- Check for alternatives to major components of the project, eg two different types of building. Set out the costs side by side, within the overall budget.

- Use BOP estimates where you have not got firm figures. A BOP estimate is your *best* (B) estimate between your most realistic *optimistic* (O) estimate and your most *pessimistic* (P) one.

- Check that nothing has been left out and that alternatives have not been ignored.

- Finally, look at the bottom line figure. Projects have a tendency to creep from sensible costings to unrealistic totals. You need to assess whether the bottom line figure appears reasonable for the project and is justified. Consider if the money could be better spent in other ways.

FUND-RAISING AND INCOME GENERATION

Q47. **What are the distinctions between fund-raising, fund development and income generation?**

A. All three involve a transaction where the school and the donor/customer feel that what they each receive is of more value than what they give.

Income generation is what it says — the generation of income from the sale of goods and services provided by the school. It is a straight commercial transaction, based on normal market considerations, although sometimes the customer may be making a generous purchase which amounts to a veiled donation.

With both *fund-raising* and *fund development* the school asks an outside person or body to donate in return for some benefit, however intangible, of at least equal value to the donor. (Often this will just be goodwill or a warm feeling for the donor!)

Fund development, however, takes a more sophisticated view of raising money, as Peter Drucker describes in *Managing the Non-Profit Organisation* (1990, Butterworth-Heinemann). There has been a shift by voluntary organisations away from using the term "fund-raising" to "fund development". Fund-raising involves requesting money because the need is great, while fund development involves creating a membership that participates through giving because they feel that the organisation deserves it.

Drucker P, *Managing the Non-Profit Organisation* (1990, Butterworth-Heinemann) deals with aspects of fund-raising and management for schools and the non-profit institutions.

> *Professional Fundraising*, published by Greenhouse Publishing, 56 Portland Road, Bishops Stortford, Herts CM23 3SJ, is a good source of up to date news and views on fund-raising.

Q48. What range of income generation is open to schools?

A.   Any or all of the following:

- sales of items produced by the school, eg food, craft goods, plants, magazines, video and audio cassettes
- sales of items bought in from outside sources, eg clothing, books and stationery, pens, etc. (This also includes commission on items sold by a third party, eg photographs.)
- the collection of coupons from sales promotions or mass entry into competitions
- sale of advertising, eg on sports strips, vehicles, and even around the school
- the sale of services, particularly but not solely from secondary schools, eg translating, language and other training, coaching, research projects, consultancy, crèche and playgroup
- the hire of facilities, eg the school buildings and grounds (including large-scale events such as rallies, residential activities and conferences), reprographic facilities, vehicles, catering
- activities and classes, eg adult classes, training, holiday schemes.

Q49. What are the advantages and disadvantages of income generation?

A.   The following potential disadvantages should be carefully considered:

- VAT should be charged in some instances and often is not (see Question 66). You may need to seek advice on this from your LEA or local VAT office
- it is important that schools are not accused of using their facilities to undercut local small businesses which ultimately help to finance them. In some cases school activities may be viewed as being unfairly competitive
- schools should be aware of the ethical issues involved: sale of goods can cause friction with parents, eg tuck-shop sales, pressure to buy items, etc
- income generation is not the school's primary purpose and could become a distraction
- additional insurance cover may be required.

Income generation can offer intangible gains such as:

- a sense of common purpose, shared enthusiasm, team-work, pupil and parent involvement
- good educational and realistic tasks for pupils to tackle.

SPECIAL EDUCATIONAL NEEDS

Q50. How should schools deal with special educational needs (SEN)?

A.   The approach to provision for pupils with special educational needs (SEN) will vary greatly from one school to another and will be different between one LEA and another. The scheme detailed below shows how the provision for SEN pupils in one LEA is tackled, but this is by no means typical.

There is provision within the Education Act 1993 for special schools to opt out of LEA control by seeking GM status either singly or in a group.

Schools are encouraged to make provision for pupils with special educational needs in their own catchment area or local area and consequently the age weighted pupil unit (AWPU) funding takes account of SEN within mainstream schools.

Provision for special educational needs is allocated under a three stage strategy.

- *Stage 1* — within the budget share of the school, 5% of the AWPU funding and 50% of the compensatory element of the formula are suggested as being allocated to provide for SEN.

- *Stage 2* — where the provision in stage 1 proves to be inadequate then resources from the Learning Support Service become available. Funding for this service is held centrally.

- *Stage 3* — if the individual needs of a pupil cannot adequately be met by the provision under stages 1 and

2, then the statementing process may be triggered, attached to which is a statutory process of assessment of need and a "value attached to the statement". Three options are then available to meet the needs of the pupil:

(i) placement in a special school

(ii) placement in a special unit attached to a mainstream school, eg units for hearing-impaired or visually-impaired pupils

(iii) placement in a mainstream school.

In each case the "value attached to the statement" is available in addition to the AWPU and compensatory elements of the school budget share.

Q51. What does the future hold for SEN funding?

A.   Delegation of budgets for special schools has so far been at the discretion of the LEA and such schools have been able to request delegation and to appeal to the Secretary of State if delegation was refused.

Under the present LMS framework, formula funding must be extended to include special schools from April 1994 and recent decisions require that full delegated powers be devolved to all special schools by April 1996. From the date of delegation funding will be place-led but will count as pupil-led for the purposes of the requirement that 80% of potential schools' budget (PSB) must be allocated on the basis of AWPUs.

From the same date LEAs will be required to delegate the cost and management to mainstream schools of special units attached to them and again these will count towards the 80% pupil-led funding requirement.

Units for excluded pupils and those for visually and hearing-impaired pupils will be exempt from this requirement, although LEAs may delegate to such units if they wish.

PAY AND PERSONNEL

Q52. What is the position regarding pay flexibility?

A.   The pay of teachers is decided by the relevant body:

- in schools without delegated budgets the LEA makes decisions on teachers' pay
- in schools with a delegated budget the governing bodies make decisions on teachers' pay and the LEA has a duty to act upon the governing bodies' decisions and make the appropriate payments to teachers
- in GM schools the relevant body is the governing body and it can apply for exemption from the provisions of the 1993 *School Teachers' Pay and Conditions Document* and fix its own pay levels and conditions for teachers in its employ. The governing body can, if it wishes, pay less than the normal scales or it can fix its own scales above the norm.

Heads and deputies — both are placed on a single pay spine with schools grouped 1–6 depending on school unit totals. Heads and deputies are paid on separate ranges on the same spine. The ranges are not incremental and there is no automatic progression through the ranges.

Certain criteria such as the difficulty filling the post, qualifications of the applicant, etc must be borne in mind when the relevant body decides where on the range a newly appointed Head or deputy is to be placed. The relevant body can move a Head or deputy up the range at its discretion and about 19.8% of Heads and 18.8% of deputies (source: Brian Clegg *Teaching Today*, NASUWT, issue

5, 1993) have benefited from discretionary progression which may be above the top of the range.

The relevant body is free to determine the number of teachers to be paid as deputy heads, having regard to the management structure which fits the needs and circumstances of the school.

Qualified teachers (classroom teachers) — the relevant body will decide how many teachers it will employ at the school having regard to needs and circumstances.

An 18 point scale has been introduced and a system of points scores took effect from 1 September 1993. Points are awarded under the following headings, with the number of points awarded determining the salary level of each individual teacher.

Points are awarded for:

- qualifications
- experience
- responsibilities
- excellence
- recruitment and retention
- special education needs.

A good honours graduate must be awarded two points (unless the resulting salary would be greater than point 9 on the teachers' pay spine), and a teacher wholly or mainly employed to teach SEN pupils must receive one point.

Apart from the above, relevant bodies have a great deal of pay flexibility in all other areas (including SEN) — see the box below.

Summary of pay flexibilities

An essential ingredient, and one that is mentioned in the 1993 *School Teachers' Pay and Conditions Document*, is the need to have in place a written, fair and open whole-school pay policy which has been arrived at after consultation with the staff.

Relevant bodies can:

- decide at which point within the range to pay Heads and deputies or to pay above the range if they wish
- decide how many, or if any, teachers shall be paid at deputy Head salary
- decide how many teachers they will employ
- decide what level and length of experience outside teaching is to be counted as qualifying for points
- decide whether or not a teacher shall be awarded a point for each year of service to the school and whether to withhold points for unsatisfactory service
- decide the number of points to award for responsibility
- award up to three points for excellence in the classroom subject to annual review
- award up to two points to holders of posts difficult to fill or in order to retain the postholder (but this situation must be reviewed every two years)
- award an extra point for qualifications in SEN and can also reward other expertise in the teaching of SEN pupils.

A great deal of responsibility has been placed on the relevant bodies when it comes to deciding the pay levels of individual teachers and the Audit Commission, in its 1993 report *Adding up the Sums*, expressed disappointment at the under-use of pay discretions by relevant bodies. Only 19.8% of Heads, 18.8% of deputies and 2.3% of other teachers were in receipt of discretionary salary enhancements.

The most serious constraint on the use of salary discretions is the size of the school budget share. Where schools have budget surpluses they are reluctant to commit them to extra salaries because of the possible long-term effects. A substantial reduction in the school budget share may make it necessary for the relevant body to consider a reduction in the number of teachers employed at the school. Employment law and redundancy procedures are an important consideration and over the past few years many schools have solved budget problems by adjusting the number of teachers employed.

Each member of the teaching staff must, from 1 September 1993, be provided with an individual salary assessment together with a job description. In fixing salary levels it is essential to refer to the relevant official documents issued by the DFE —*School Teachers' Pay and Conditions Document* and Circular 8/93.

School Teachers' Review Body Second Report (1993, HMSO).

School Teachers' Pay and Conditions Document (1993, DFE).

Circular 8/93 — School Teachers' Pay and Conditions of Employment, DFE.

A Whole School Pay Policy, 1991, NAGM/AGIT (amended 1993).

Local Government Act 1988 (Defined Activities) (Exemptions) (Small Schools) Order 1992 (SI 1992 No.1626).

Q53. Will performance related pay ever become a reality?

A. The possible introduction of a scheme of performance related pay (PRP) was part of the remit of the Secretary of State to the School Teachers' Review Body (STRB) when it was established in 1991.

The DFE submission of evidence to the STRB made it clear that the Secretary of State was interested in a scheme that related teachers' pay to individual performance and that such a scheme should form an essential component in all governing bodies' pay policies (but without providing any additional resources to finance such a scheme).

The STRB favoured a scheme of PRP based on the performance of the whole school rather than on the individual teacher. The STRB, having consulted widely with large organisations operating PRP schemes, identified certain key elements in such schemes:

- they are more likely to be successful when the basic salary structure and levels of pay are regarded as fair

- most successful schemes had begun with senior management and applied gradually down the organisation

- the majority of staff should see the possibility of higher pay for improved performance and not just the "high fliers"

- without exception, a PRP scheme resulted in an initial increase in the salary bill and was considered a necessary investment.

In a second report, published in 1993, the STRB, though still favouring its original proposal for PRP based on whole-school performance, recognised the determination of the Secretary of State's preference for the individual teacher approach. Three major factors are apparent:

- the impact on teacher appraisal, which was originally intended to inform teachers of their professional development (a teacher with a favourable appraisal report will be more likely to receive a pay award for performance than one who cannot produce such evidence)

- the development of reliable performance indicators which will measure the "value added" factor
- the need for additional funding at least in the initial period.

Both sides of the debate have decided on pilot schemes. The Secretary of State has invited schools to bid to take part in the DFE scheme and will choose 12 schools. The STRB has decided to pilot a scheme in 20 schools aimed at examining ways of rewarding Heads and deputies on a performance related basis.

The STRB is attempting to ride both horses since a major criterion in its scheme is likely to be the performance of the school as a whole. What seems likely is that the Secretary of State will attempt to press ahead with a full blown scheme of "merit money" based on the individual performance of teachers in spite of opposition from teacher unions and a boycott of the scheme promised by some.

It is difficult to see how governing bodies will be able to include PRP in pay policies without an increase in schools' budgets. The bottom line of any policy is likely to read "PRP will be introduced as and when extra resources become available".

ASSOCIATE STAFF/VOLUNTEERS

Q54. What should the school bursar's role be?

A. The term *bursar* has no strict definition. However, in secondary schools the normal full role is a managerial one and usually the bursar is a member of the senior management team. The bursar is usually responsible for:
- finance (budget, financial management, purchasing)
- office management
- personnel management of all associate staff

- premises and grounds, furniture and fittings
- health and safety
- transport
- catering
- clerking of the governing body (possibly).

This role largely corresponds to that in the independent schools, although there the bursar can sometimes be almost independent of the Head and answerable directly to the governors.

The key requirements for a bursar are:

- a good job specification
- a clear *managerial* role
- sufficient administrative back-up with supporting staff and facilities.

Not many primary schools have appointed bursars. There are, however a growing number of bursars serving a group or cluster of primary schools.

Q55. **How can imaginative use of associate (non-teaching) staff improve a school's cost-efficiency?**

A. The term "associate staff" has recently been advocated by Professor Mortimore and his team (details below) as being more positive and comprehensive than "non-teaching" or "support" staff.

In today's environment there are an emerging range of factors affecting schools:

- the growing emphasis of management in schools — both educational research and Government policy stress the importance of management for school effectiveness
- the increased responsibilities which schools have assumed — many arising out of LMS such as planning, financial management, PR and marketing, personnel

management, use of information technology for management, servicing the governing body, informing parents, working with the community, etc

- the growing pressure on teachers created by the National Curriculum and national schemes of assessment.

All of these factors are creating acute time-management problems. They are also creating skill-management problems, in that Heads, deputies and other staff are being asked to use skills for which they have never been trained and which they may not possess.

In this context it is logical for schools to look more closely at the use of associate staff, because they often possess a wider range of skills and experience, and also because they are often less costly to employ. Associate staff may be able to provide the same service at less cost, or an extended service at the same cost.

There are a whole range of areas where associate staff can be, and often are, employed:

- finance and resources
- premises and grounds
- personnel management
- health and safety
- public relations and communications
- fund-raising and marketing
- pupil registration, attendance and records
- secretarial services
- examination administration, etc.

Such staff may be dedicated to a particular function, but often are employed in a managerial capacity, eg a bursar, finance officer, office and IT manager, premises manager or business manager/fund-raiser.

Recently a very useful study by Professor Peter Mortimore and colleagues for the DFE has given detailed case studies of more innovative examples, with their costs (see below). The examples include both managerial posts, such as those above, and posts at a lower level, eg providing classroom support. Frequently, examples are given of an increase in cost-efficiency, eg employing an associate at a substantially reduced cost per hour to administer school examinations; or in cost-effectiveness, eg employing a bursar to co-ordinate and plan improvements to the school environment. The study advocates a comprehensive review of *all* personnel functions in the school, creating a multi-disciplinary team of both teachers and a range of associates.

Schools wishing to explore these possibilities would be wise to adopt a systematic approach, as follows:

- conduct a SWOT analysis of the present staffing structure and organisation — its strengths and weaknesses, opportunities and threats

- conduct a personnel audit — this needs a comprehensive review of all personnel, teachers and associates, who have responsibilities other than teaching. For each individual you need to record:

  - salary

  - hours per week and weeks per annum worked

  - main weekly tasks (both teaching and non-teaching)

  - major seasonal (ie not every week) tasks

  - extra skills needed for these tasks (beyond those currently possessed)

  - skills not currently used

- conduct a task analysis — identify the tasks, other than teaching, that need to be done (some may be covered at present, some not) and the skills needed

- devise an action plan to modify the personnel structure, deployment and training, to fit the tasks needed.

Mortimore P and J, with Thomas H, *The Innovative Use of Non-Teaching Staff in Primary and Secondary Schools Project: Final Report* (1992, DFE), and a more recent version, *Managing Associate Staff* (1993, Paul Chapman). See also HMI, *Non-Teaching Staff in Schools* (1992, HMSO).

Q56. How can the value of volunteers be maximised?

A. Volunteers are an enormous potential asset to schools — far more valuable than is often assumed. Suppose the Secretary of State offered to fund your school for additional associate staff with total weekly hours equivalent to total weekly teacher contract hours. In an average size primary school this would amount to 200 hours or so per week; in a secondary school to over 1000 hours per week. The value would be equivalent to around 25% of the school's total budget. Would you accept the offer? Most schools would find it one too good to refuse — though they would then need to rethink fundamentally how they would use this associate staff time.

Now suppose the Secretary of State has a change of mind and withdraws the offer, but points out that you only need to employ a part-time volunteer organiser for perhaps 10 hours per week to raise this huge and very valuable resource for yourself. There are volunteers out in your community, if only they can be found and organised. Faced with such a valuable asset, would it not make sense for your school to acquire it?

As a resource, volunteers bring the same advantages as associate staff — a wider range of experience and skills. Indeed, potentially, they cover a much wider range, from senior executive to manual worker. Just look at the jobs volunteers already do in many communities — organisers, co-ordinators, managers, treasurers, project-leaders, trainers, teamleaders, secretaries, clerks, craftsmen and women, artists, etc. In addition, they bring other benefits:

- they improve the adult-to-child ratio
- they act as goodwill ambassadors in the community
- they are free — or nearly so.

Of course, volunteers should be regarded as a complementary and not as a cheap alternative to salaried staff. They do also have limitations. They are not employed on contracts. They *can* sometimes let you down, or try to take over. But this is much less likely to happen if they are properly inducted, trained, monitored — and thanked!

Peter Drucker stresses that the key to enlisting the full value of volunteers is to treat volunteers as "unpaid members" of the organisation. To achieve this organisations should set a framework so that volunteers optimise their satisfaction from their contribution. This is more likely to be achieved if organisations specify volunteers' job descriptions and targets and provide training. So to maximise volunteers you need this kind of view of their role.

An audit is a good starting point to determine all the possible tasks in your organisation which *could* be done by the right volunteers. The next point to be determined is how you are going to "manage" volunteers. A Head, heads of departments, or classteachers can cope with a volunteer here and there, but if you are serious about recruiting volunteers *en masse*, then someone has to have their management as a key task. The ideal is to fund from the budget a part-time volunteer co-ordinator — perhaps with a salary linked to the weekly volunteer hours achieved. Given the right person this is a better proposition than expecting a busy Head or deputy to perform this task, or giving an allowance to a teacher who is tied to the classroom just at the time volunteers will be most active.

The "volunteer manager" will have plenty to do:
- recruitment (largely by word of mouth)
- induction and training
- briefing of teachers and other staff
- sensitive monitoring and trouble-shooting
- giving rewards or praise.

There will also be the question of developing a positive and sensitive attitude among teaching staff, perhaps through an INSET session.

Maximising volunteers' value effectively is not a simple bolt-on process. It requires rethinking the school's attitude to volunteers and its management of them. However, the effective use of volunteers offers the potential of significant financial benefits.

Q57. How can pupils be involved in LMS?

A.   If the school is now managing itself, it seems logical to involve pupils in that management. There are a number of examples now of pupil involvement in both primary and secondary schools — providing ideas and sharing in decisions, making surveys or studies, or providing labour. The following areas could benefit from pupil involvement:
- energy management — a number of schools have organised pupils to monitor the temperature and behaviour

of heating systems; many others have enlisted their support in energy saving campaigns

- reporting defects — some schools have a defects book in which pupils can report defects in premises, furniture and fittings, grounds, etc

- maintenance — there are examples of involvement of pupils in discussion of priorities or choice of colours in redecoration; secondary schools have often organised groups of students for redecoration of classrooms, either as part of a pre-vocational course or as volunteers

- cleaning — in some European countries and in Japan pupils are responsible for the cleaning of their classrooms

- grounds maintenance — independent schools sometimes have "estate work" as an afternoon option

- minor improvements — some schools have allocated funds to year-groups or the school council, for premises and grounds improvements or furniture purchases; others have enlisted pupils to raise funds for these

- business studies and economic awareness — some schools have used the school budget as curriculum material for this area

- fund-raising — here pupils have traditionally been heavily involved, particularly in fund-raising events

- income generation — again a traditional involvement (selling and producing items, etc), but more recent examples in secondary schools include research, surveys and development projects.

In general, it looks as if there is still scope in many schools for increasing the involvement of pupils in LMS, both to assist the school's finances and improve its operation, and as a worthwhile educational experience, but of course there can be ethical, health and safety issues, etc.

CONTRACTS AND COMPULSORY COMPETITIVE TENDERING

Q58. What is compulsory competitive tendering (CCT)?

A.   CCT was introduced in order to allow private companies to bid for work which was traditionally carried out by employees of the local authority and to allow schools with delegated budgets the freedom to draw up their own specifications for certain work in order to obtain value for money.

School cleaning, meals, grounds maintenance, vehicle repair and servicing are all *defined activities* under the terms of s.2 of the Local Government Act 1988, and as such are subject to competitive tendering legislation.

Q59. How does CCT affect maintained schools?

A.   For the purposes of school cleaning and grounds maintenance, CCT does not apply to small schools where it is estimated that not more than three full-time employees will be required to carry out the work.

When LMS was introduced into schools, contracts for the defined activities were placed by the LEA and some or all of these contracts have come up for renewal.

When contracts are due to be renewed several options are available to the school.
1. It can continue to participate in the next LEA contract which is subject to CCT legislation.
2. It can organise its own contract, which can be done in one of three ways:

(a) by setting up its own "in-house" direct service organisation (DSO) (schools should ensure that the client role is kept totally separate from that of a contractor)
(b) by inviting tenders from various contractors, including the DSO of the LEA
(c) by dealing directly with private contractors.

In the case of option 1, the LEA will draw up the specification of the service to form part of the contract. The school will have an opportunity to modify the specification to suit its particular needs and in the light of experience gained over the previous contract period. The LEA may accept the modified specification and include it in the contract. Alternatively, the LEA may consider the modifications unreasonable, in which case the school will be asked to vary its specification or arrange its own contract.

So far as option 2 is concerned, by setting up its own in-house organisation the school *must* comply with competitive tendering legislation, whether or not the DSO is invited to tender for the work. If the same staff who were previously employed under the DSO are re-employed to do the same work, but for a private contractor, then under the terms of an EC Directive (which has yet to be tested in the UK courts) they would be entitled to the *same or better* pay and conditions as they previously enjoyed when employed by the DSO. (This may have some effect on the number of contractors wishing to tender for work in schools.)

If the school were to negotiate its own contract with private contractors, CCT would *not* apply, but four important factors need to be taken into account. The school:

• must comply with the LEA regulations and standing orders on tendering
• must manage the contract during its duration

- must accept the financial outcomes
- cannot then ask the LEA to do the work (if things go wrong) until the LEA contract comes up for renewal.

See below for a step-by-step guide to the options above.

Step-by-step guide to CCT for maintained schools

1. School decides to stay with LEA contract (CCT applies)

School

LEA

- Consults school on level of service, ie draft specification

- Accepts or modifies draft specification

- Draws up specification and contract

- Decides who to include in list of contractors

- Draws up list of contractors

- Checks list of contractors

- Invites tenders and awards contract

- Decides which personnel will work at the school

- Monitors and administers the contract

2(a). School decides to set up its own DSO (CCT applies)

In this case the school has a dual role.

School   **DSO**

- Sets up the DSO
- Prepares specification and
  contract (expert advice may be
  needed)
- Draws up list of contractors
  from approved list
- Invites tenders and awards contracts • Prepares tender
- Monitors and administers the contract • Operates contract if awarded

NB. Problems could arise if, in future years the school DSO fails to win the contract.

2(b). School invites tenders from contractors, including the LEA and DSO. (DSO bound by LEA tendering regulations and standing orders.)

School

- Prepares specification and contract (expert advice may be needed)
- Draws up list of contractors
- Invites tenders and awards contract
- Monitors and administers the contract

2(c). School decides on private contractor (CCT does not apply)

Local Management in Schools and Compulsory Competition, an occasional paper produced by the Chartered Institute of Public Finance and Accountancy (CIPFA)

Realising the Benefits of Competition, Audit Commission (1993, HMSO)

Circular 7/88, *Education Reform Act 1988: Local Management of Schools*

Q60. What is the case regarding CCT and GM or voluntary-aided schools?

A.   Once a school is granted GM status it is free to deal with its own contracts for cleaning and grounds maintenance. If a private contractor is used then CCT does *not* apply unless the DSO is invited to tender. The provision of services by DSOs will be subject to a time limit when a section of the Education Act 1993 becomes operative by order of the Secretary of State.

Voluntary-aided schools can arrange their own contracts without reference to CCT unless they invite tenders from the DSO.

Q61. What are the factors to take into account when purchasing and entering into contracts?

A.   Contracts for the supply of goods and services to maintained schools can be arranged through the central supplies organisation of most LEAs. Maintained schools are not obliged to use the central supplies organisation, though most primary schools do, but a school would be wise to at least check the service that is available.

Using a central supplies organisation has the advantage that expert staff, well-experienced in quality control and the placing of large contracts, are often able to negotiate competitive prices.

Contracts for supplies and services to GM schools can be made with the LEA but when an order is made under the Education Act 1993 this practice will be limited to a period of two years, after which time these schools must negotiate their own contracts (often with the same supplier).

Before entering into any contractual arrangement schools should have regard to the following factors:

• price — comparisons between prices quoted by LEA central supplies, in trade journals and in education suppliers' catalogues, etc will have to be made

• quality — a certain minimum quality standard should form part of the specification

- reliability — goods that fail to stand up to the wear and tear of school use do not represent value for money
- after-sales services — a section should deal with the question of repair and/or servicing and replacement particularly if the item is a vital piece of equipment and is in frequent use. (Care should be taken with contract hire arrangements, especially for computer networks and reprographic equipment.)
- value for money — all the above factors should be governed by the need to obtain value for money. Though price is an important element in negotiating a contract it should not be allowed to dominate the contract at the expense of other equally important factors.

Buying for Quality. Free from DFE Publications Centre. Prepared by Coopers and Lybrand for the School Management Task Force 1992.

Q62. What are the procedures involved when purchasing or entering into contracts?

A. The first thing to do is to formulate a written code of practice which should not be deviated from without very good reasons. The following points form the basis on which a sound purchasing policy could be formulated.

Procedures for the ordering of goods/services should conform to the financial regulations and standing orders of the funding-provider for the particular type of school (LEAs for maintained schools, the DFE for GM schools). Such regulations will normally contain the following, or similar guidelines.

Value of goods/service	Procedure
Up to £x	No need to obtain written quotations but best value for money is necessary.
£x to £y	Three competitive written quotations must be obtained except in special circumstances. Governing body approval is required.
Over £z	Must be advertised publicly or contractors must be invited to tender from an LEA approved list.

- Ideally three persons should be authorised to order, receive goods and certify invoices for payment. Each authorised person should be allocated a separate function.

- Orders should be made out on official forms, specially printed for the purpose, and numbered and dated.

- When not in use, order forms should be kept in a secure, locked location.

- Telephone orders should always be confirmed in writing on an official order form.

- Whenever possible, goods delivered to the school should always be checked before signing the delivery note. (Otherwise, it is wise to sign the delivery note "unexamined", especially if a large consignment is delivered and the goods are packaged.)

- Goods should not be left in the school entrance after delivery but should be moved to a secure store or sent to the appropriate department.

- Official records of all transactions should be maintained and amounts debited against the appropriate department's capitation allowance.

SPREADSHEETS

Q63. What is a spreadsheet?

A.   A *spreadsheet* is a computerised combination of a very large piece of paper and a multi-function calculator. Its format is a grid of rows and columns. The point at which a row and a column intersect is known as a cell. Each cell is uniquely indexed and information is stored in cells either as text, numbers or formulae.

A typical spreadsheet would look like this.

	A	B	C	D	E	F	G
1	Teaching staff	200,000					
2	A P T & C staff	25,000					
3	Hourly-paid staff	20,000					
4	TOTAL	245,000						← A cell (G4)
5							
6							
7							
8							
9							
10							

Well-known spreadsheet packages include Lotus 1-2-3, Microsoft Excel and SuperCalc.

Q64. What are the advantages of a spreadsheet?

A.   The main advantage of a spreadsheet over manual calculation or more traditional methods is its capacity, speed and consistency. Changes to any of the information stored in the cells is immediately and automatically reflected in the other cells without the user having to rework results, such as totals or percentages. However, it must be remembered that a spreadsheet is only a tool and as with manual calculations, accuracy depends on the user.

Q65.   What are the main uses of a spreadsheet?

A.   Spreadsheets are used as:

- *worksheets* to perform calculations
- *databases* to store, sort, extract and analyse data quickly
- *charts and graphics* to present information in an easily understood way.

Worksheets can be used for calculations from simple arithmetic to multi-linked financial models and can include mathematical, statistical, financial, matrix, trigonometric and logical functions. They are best used for dealing with large or complex calculations where manual recalculation would be time-consuming, or for modelling, where the effect of changes in one area on another are required.

Modelling deals with situations where there are too many variables to calculate manually and where answers to the question "What if?" are required quickly. This can be done by linking different calculations together either on a single worksheet, with multiple worksheets or even different file documents (see the box on following page).

Example of how documents link together on a computer system

Salary Scales Table

	£
8	16,576
9	17,760
10	18,942
Head 13	24,702
Deputy 4	23,505

This "lookup" table represents a database of salary scale points which may be selected in a calculation area. When the table is updated for pay rises, any linked calculations will also be changed.

Staff calculation area

		£
Head	13	24,702
Deputy	4	23,505
Teacher	10	18,942
Teacher	9	17,760
Sub total		84,909
Oncosts	15%	12,736
Total		97,645

The correct salary is automatically selected from the lookup table by inserting the scale point.

The oncost % is a factor which may change.

Premises costs

	£
Repairs	5,000
Gas	3,000
Electricity	2,000
Water	2,000
Rates	5,000
Total premises	17,000

This is an example of a working paper which links to the summary. Individual alterations will change the page total and also the summary total.

Summary		
	£	
Teaching staff costs	97,645	The summary is fed by a
Non teaching	11,500	number of working
Premises	17,000	papers. Any changes
Capitation	5,000	made in the working
		papers will recalculate the
		summary.
Total	131,145	

A *database* stores interrelated data in list form. The data can be sorted into different orders or parts can be extracted to provide information for the user. Where users require different information from the same basic set of data, a well prepared database can save duplication of effort. For example, lists of pupil names, surnames, dates of birth and classes could be sorted into alphabetical order within each class, alphabetically for the whole school, by age within class or within the school.

Schools often hold information on database programs which are more powerful than spreadsheet databases. Data can be transferred from these programs onto spreadsheets in order to perform calculations. This saves duplication of input and improves consistency by sharing the same set of data.

Reports showing only lists of numbers are not the only way of presenting information. Spreadsheets contain a wide range of *charts and graphics* to enhance the reporting of information.

Different graphs, bar charts and pie diagrams are available to represent information pictorially calculated on the worksheets. These are especially useful for comparisons and summaries (see below).

Many spreadsheets contain graphics functions for changing the size and type of text, drawing borders, shading, and adding drawings to reports. This improves the quality and therefore the potential impact of a report.

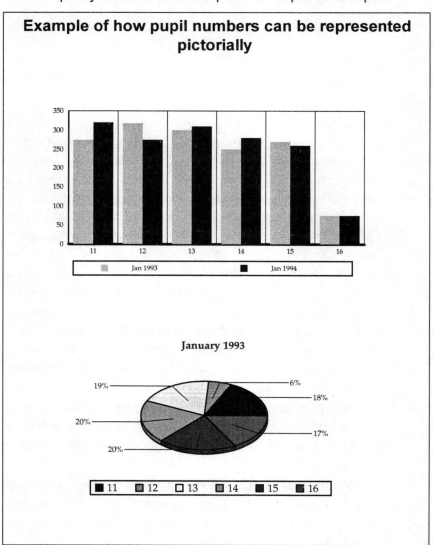

Example of how pupil numbers can be represented pictorially

January 1993

TAX

Q66. **In education, which goods and services are subject to Value Added Tax (VAT) and which are not?**

A.   It is only possible to deal with VAT in a general way and if you require detailed information or answers to specific questions then seek the help of your LEA or local VAT office (the number is available from your local telephone directory).

Basically, the position as far as education is concerned is covered by exemption 6, group 6 of schedule 6, of the Value Added Tax Act 1983. This extract from the Act is printed in the back of VAT leaflet 701/30/87, obtainable from your local VAT office.

If a local authority or other persons provide education — free of cost or for a fee that is less than cost — the supply of education is not a business activity and is outside the scope of VAT.

For a fee at or above cost, the supply is a business activity and is treated in the same way as similar supplies made in the private sector.

The exemption for schools covers:
- registered schools
- GM schools
- voluntary-aided schools
- voluntary-controlled schools
- special agreement schools.

The relief does not extend to education which includes provision of tuition in, or facilities for, recreation and sport except as part of a general education curriculum.

Individual private tuition (except sporting and recreation) is exempt from VAT even if provided for profit as long as the tutor is acting on his or her own behalf and not for an employer or organisation.

Marking of examination papers for examination boards by teachers and similar persons is standard-rated if the person supplying the service is a VAT taxable person.

In general, visits organised by schools for their own pupils are exempt if the visit is related to the schools' curriculum, eg field trips and visits to museums.

Holidays, including for example adventure courses, are liable to VAT.

The sale of materials to pupils is exempt from VAT provided the sale is made as part of a course of exempt education, eg pens, books, mathematical instruments, craft materials. If however these sales are made through shops owned and operated by the school then they are subject to VAT.

VAT Leaflets 701/30/87, 706/1992, 708/1/90, HM Customs and Excise.

Q67. How is VAT reclaimed?

A.   In almost every case, the VAT paid on invoices for goods and/or services supplied to a school will be reclaimed by the LEA from Customs and Excise. Other schools registered for VAT will be able to reclaim VAT paid on invoices for supplies of goods and/or services. Similarly, VAT charged on invoices raised by the school will need to be paid over to Customs and Excise.

GM schools not registered for VAT, ie with a turnover of less than £37,600 are not able to reclaim VAT and therefore they receive a special purpose grant, amounting to 2.5% of their annual maintenance grant (less the reduction in rates liability because they are exempt charities), to compensate for this.

Q68. What is the difference between input and output tax?

A. If you make standard-rated supplies you have to account to Customs and Excise for the tax due. This is your *output* tax. Normally you charge the tax to your customers. If your customers are registered for VAT and the supplies from you are used in their businesses the tax you charge is their *input* tax. Supplies that you purchase for use in your business on which you pay tax is your *input* tax.

LEAs will have financial procedures to deal with input and output VAT and these are designed to ensure that they avoid unnecessary payment of tax; schools should be familiar with the procedures and follow them to the letter.

Premises run for educational purposes have no VAT charged but if they are used outside school hours, eg for a creche or other commercial purpose, then up to 5% of the VAT on those services can be reclaimed for general over-head costs.

Q69. What is the Construction Industry Tax Deduction Scheme (CITDS)?

A. The Construction Industry Tax Deduction Scheme (CITDS) was introduced by the Inland Revenue to ensure that self-employed subcontractors in the construction industry paid tax at the appropriate rate — and that tax avoidance was not encouraged by loop-holes in procedures.

The regulations are specific and easy to implement. When an LEA, GM or independent school engages a builder, for example on site preparation, alteration, construction or repair, it assumes the role of "contractor". As such it must deduct tax at the basic rate (25% at the time of writing) from all payments (excluding the cost of materials) for work undertaken by a subcontractor, unless the latter can prove that such a deduction should not be made by producing a subcontractor's certificate provided by the Inland Revenue. A special concession covers operations amounting to less than £250, but before this can be invoked, suitable arrangements must be made by the contractor with the Tax Office. VAT should be excluded when calculating the amount to be deducted from payments. A contractor must register with the local Tax Office when it engages a subcontractor, so that all the necessary documentation for the proper payment of tax deducted can be obtained.

A subcontractor's certificate is issued by the Inland Revenue and contains a photograph of the subcontractor on the front and his or her signature on the back. The onus is on the contractor to verify the identity of the subcontractor, his or her signature and to check whether the certificate is valid. The contractor should be fully satisfied on all counts, before authorising payment without the deduction of tax. (Remember — if you do not carry out these checks the school may have to pay the deduction!)

When payment has been made without the deduction of tax, the subcontractor will provide the contractor with a voucher certifying receipt of the gross payment, which the contractor must submit to the Inland Revenue. Full details of the scheme are available from the Inland Revenue on request (booklet IR14/15 — *Construction Tax Deduction Scheme*).